Falling Asleep in the Lap of Delilah

Lessons on Finishing Well from the Life of Samson

By Philip E. Morrison

OASIS

Falling Asleep in the Lap of Delilah

Copyright © 2018 Philip E. Morrison

All rights reserved. No part of this publication may be reproduced or transmitted in any form or by any means, electronic or mechanical, including photocopy, recording, or any information storage and retrieval system, except for brief quotations in printed reviews, without the prior permission of the author or publisher.

ISBN 13: 978-1-59452-748-7
ISBN: 1-59452-748-2

Published by Oasis International, Ltd. in partnership with Phil Morrison. To find out more about Phil and his ministry, contact him at philjanmorrison@gmail.com.

Oasis International is a ministry devoted to fostering a robust and sustainable pan-African publishing industry. For more information, go to oasisint.net.

Unless otherwise noted, Scripture taken from the HOLY BIBLE, NEW INTERNATIONAL VERSION®. NIV®. Copyright © 1973, 1978, 1984, 2011 by International Bible Society. Used by permission of Zondervan. All rights reserved worldwide.

Scripture quotations from the ESV® Bible (The Holy Bible, English Standard Version®), copyright © 2001 by Crossway, a publishing ministry of Good News Publishers. Used by permission. All rights reserved."

Cover art: Rubens, Samson and Delilah, c. 1609-10. https://www.nationalgallery.org.uk/paintings/learn-about-art/lives-of-artists/rubens-a-master-in-the-making?viewPage=5

18 19 20 21 22 23 BPI 6 5 4 3 2 1

Other Books by Philip E. Morrison

The Multi-Church Pastor

Questions Pastors Ask

Seven Surprises for the Pastor

Conflict Resolution in the Church

Stewardship of Time

Influence: Leading Without Position

For Our Children! For Our Church!

DEDICATION

This book is dedicated to my father, Ross I. Morrison, Sr. and my mother June D. Morrison who are still running their races in their 90's. They are continuing to set an outstanding example of finishing well and are sterling examples of what the Psalmist describes:

> The righteous will flourish like a palm tree, they will grow like a cedar of Lebanon; planted in the house of the Lord, they will flourish in the courts of our God. They will still bear fruit in old age, they will stay fresh and green (Psalm 92:12-14).

Thank you, Dad and Mom, for showing us the way!

CONTENTS

Other books by Philip E. Morrison	iii
Dedication	v
Table of Contents	vii
Acknowledgements	ix
Foreword	xi
Preface	xvii
Prologue	1
Chapter One: The Issue of Spiritual Coldness or "Falling Asleep in the Lap of Delilah"	3
Chapter Two: The Issue of Compromise	15
Chapter Three: The Issue of Authenticity – Resisting Secretive and Deceptive Living.	23
Chapter Four: The Issue of Revenge	35
Chapter Five: The Issue of Purity	43
Chapter Six: The Issue of Isolation	65
Chapter Seven: The Loss of Spiritual Power	73
Chapter Eight: The Issue of Concentration	79
Chapter Nine: The Issue of Drift	87
Chapter Ten: The Issue of Intentionality or The End Is the Beginning	95
Epilogue	105
Finishing Well Questionnaire	111
Works Cited	113

ACKNOWLEDGEMENTS

Thanks to my wife, Jan, my life partner and friend, who knows my struggles and weakness better than anyone and yet loves me anyway! Thank you for over four decades of love and support and for your patience with me in this and many other projects. With your encouragement I hope to finish well.

Thanks to my daughter, Katie, for her careful reading of the manuscript, editorial corrections, and her helpful insights and suggestions.

Thanks to George Renner for his friendship and mentoring over the past 20-plus years. Thanks for your encouragement on this and other projects over the years. A special thank you for taking the time to read the manuscript and for writing the Foreword.

Thanks to Africa Inland Mission leadership, on many levels, who have given me the freedom to pursue this and other writing projects. Your support has been a great encouragement.

Finally, thanks to Jesus Christ, my Lord and Saviour, for the highest example of finishing well. As the author of the book of Hebrews wrote, "who for the joy that was set before him endured the cross, despising the shame, and is set down at the right hand of the throne of God" (Hebrews 12:2, KJV). To him be the praise, honour, and glory forever and ever!

FOREWORD

Over and over, God implores us in his Word to do whatever it takes to find wisdom. So we read exhortations like this throughout the Proverbs of Solomon:

> Good friend, take to heart what I'm telling you; collect my counsels and guard them with your life. Tune your ears to the world of Wisdom; set your heart on a life of Understanding (Proverbs 2:1-2, The Message).

Inspired by the Holy Spirit, the writers of Scripture can't seem to say enough about the benefits of gaining wisdom:

> You're blessed when you meet Lady Wisdom, when you make friends with Madame Insight. She's worth far more than money in the bank; her friendship is better than a big salary. Her value exceeds all the trappings of wealth; nothing you could wish for holds a candle to her. With one hand she gives long life, with the other she confers recognition. Her manner is beautiful, her life wonderfully complete. She's the very Tree of Life to those who embrace her. Hold her tight – and be blessed!

> Dear friend, guard Clear Thinking and Common Sense with your life; don't for a minute lose sight of them. They'll keep your soul alive and well, they'll keep you fit and attractive. You'll travel safely, you'll neither tire nor trip. You'll take afternoon naps without a worry, you'll enjoy a good night's sleep. No need to panic over alarms or surprises, or predictions that doomsday's just around the

corner, Because GOD will be right there with you; he'll keep you safe and sound (Proverbs 3:13-18, 21-26, The Message).

To happen upon and read Phil Morrison's newest book, *Falling Asleep in the Lap of Delilah: Lessons on Finishing Well from the Life of Samson* is to discover a treasure trove of wisdom.

I regard Phil as a wise counsellor and friend. He's a veteran pastor and educator and a long-time missionary with Africa Inland Mission. *Falling Asleep in the Lap of Delilah* is a bit like the reflections found in the biblical book, Ecclesiastes. Phil offers us a series of meditations on the life of Israel's (in)famous judge, Samson, the notorious long-haired strong-man. The insights contained in this small book are grounded in thoughtful meditation of the Word of God. Anyone who desires wisdom can benefit from Phil's insights, although the primary focus is on pastors who are closing in on the final season of ministry. The chapters contain a feast of quotations from many diverse sources. But Phil's writing is not abstract or theoretical. He's speaking to us out of his own life experience.

Phil adopts a metaphor which expresses the tragic outcome that many long-serving Christians experience in the second half of life and ministry. He uses the metaphor, drawn from Samson's life, of "Delilah's lap". Phil says, "Delilah's lap represents the deceptive and deceitful claims to comfort and inner peace that the Devil offers to us in our times of inner turmoil and anxiety. But it is a false comfort."

For me, reading Phil's book was a very searching personal experience. I'm entering the final third of life and am deeply committed to finishing well. So the counsel and warnings that Phil offers are very welcome. One of the aspects of the book that make the sobering warnings more readily accepted is that Phil does not lord it over his readers or teach like the Pharisees that Jesus rejects in Matthew 23. Phil is transparent throughout and shares from his own journey and challenges in ministry. He does not hide behind his significant ministry accomplishments. On the contrary, he invites us to struggle along with him in facing the temptations common to man. We read paragraphs like this one throughout the book:

> Over the years, I have struggled with truthful living because I was addicted to projecting a perfect image. As a pastor, I could never be wrong or make a mistake. As a husband I was defensive of any criticism because I had to look good. As a father, it affected how I disciplined my children because their behaviour reflected on me. It wasn't until God brought me to Africa that I met another missionary who gently confronted me with my deceptive lifestyle.
>
> I resisted at first, and he told me later that I was the hardest case he had ever encountered. I was a pastor, a missionary, and totally living in a self-deceptive world of trying to project an image of myself that was not spiritually authentic. Others could see it; I could not until God in his grace broke through.

Phil Morrison is the real deal. This is what he's like in face-to-face conversation.

Anyone with his or her eyes open will certainly affirm the urgency of a book on finishing well. I know too many of my age-mates whose final years leading up to retirement involve a deteriorating quality of living. Far too many who began well become obsessed with the trivial, if not blatantly immoral. For most men, realizing that the end of one's career is approaching is a terrifying awareness. Often we try to deny this. Our therapeutic culture abets my neurosis. On those rare occasions when I allow the reality of the end of my professional life to enter my consciousness, it normally instils fear. And fear (as Phil explains) can cause us to do negative things to cope.

Phil proposes that one of the factors that can propel us into Delilah's lap is our search for an antidote to inner pain. He says, "I believe a primary reason [*driving Samson*] was the need to be comforted. The opposite of comfort is pain." Pain comes in so many forms. But there is a common existential pain experienced by most men in the second half of life. It is the effect of the fear expressed in Psalm 71:9: "Do not cast me away when I am old; do not forsake me when my strength is gone." We may have our doctrine correct and be assured of our salvation. But the fear of the loss of identity and of significance experienced by many is still painful. It can feel as if God has cast us away. Fear of being cast away from the ministry that has defined our lives can disrupt our best intentions to finish well.

The concern to finish well and not experience what holocaust survivor Elie Wiesel referred to as death before death, is not a recent phenomenon. Professor Wiesel said, "Because of indifference, one dies before one actually dies." One of the early church fathers, Hermas, exhorted one of his friends in these words:

> Your spirit is now old and withered up and has lost its power in consequence of your infirmities and doubts. For, like elderly men who have no hope of renewing their strength, and expect nothing but their last sleep, so you, weakened by worldly occupations, have given yourself up to sloth, and have not cast your cares upon the Lord. Your spirit therefore is broken, and you have grown old in your sorrows (*The Shepherd of Hermas*).

Hermas describes what for many of us is our worst nightmare – the shrivelling up of the person and his relationship to God, even though his physical existence continues. I agree with Norman Cousins. He said, "Death is not the greatest loss in life. The greatest loss is what dies inside us while we live." Phil Morrison's counsel can guide us as we see the final third of life approaching. Phil definitely agrees with the writer of Psalm 92. He presents for us a way to persevere in our relationship with the Lord and with others. Like the Psalm-writer, Phil affirms,

> The righteous will flourish like a palm tree, they will grow like a cedar of Lebanon; planted in the house of the Lord, will flourish in the courts of our God.They will still bear fruit in old age, they will stay fresh and green (Psalm 92:12-14).

Phil knows that in the Lord there is hope for each of us to live a life that continues to flourish into old age. But he discerningly issues a series of strong warnings and pleads with us to avoid the paths that can lead to ruin and deterioration. One powerful insight that Phil gives us is the warning about an attitude of exemption. As we pass through the prime of our ministry years and experience some measure of success in God's work we can fall prey to a seductive temptation. Phil's counsel is exactly that given by the Apostle Paul to his friends in 1 Corinthians 10:11-12: "These things happened to them as examples and were written down as warnings for us, on whom the fulfilment of the ages has come. So, if you think you are standing firm, be careful that you don't fall!" I am personally much more attentive to the perils of spiritual leadership now that I have read *Falling Asleep in the Lap of Delilah*.

Phil also wisely observes that for many (most?) people the process of decline is usually not a huge catastrophe, but what Oswald Chambers called "spiritual leakage". As Phil expresses it, "Slowly the spiritual pressure seeps out of one's life and their relationship with the Lord goes flat." Phil offers great insight to help us diagnose "how the bright embers of enthusiasm fade".

I am going to take action in response to some of Phil's counsel. One step I am working on since reading this book is reconnecting with an accountability partner. Phil warns us about isolation in chapter six and urges every spiritual leader (in fact, every Christ-follower!) to be in at least one relationship in which there is radical transparency. Phil urges that such a spiritual friendship is a key way in which we fulfil the exhortation of the writer of Hebrews 3:12-13: "See to it brothers, that none of you has a sinful, unbelieving heart that turns away from the living God. But encourage one another daily, as long as it is called Today, so that none of you may be hardened by sins deceitfulness."

I am also planning to use the helpful "Finishing Well Questionnaire" that's found at the end of this book. It's a helpful tool for self-examination and life planning.

I also want to affirm Phil's **grace** emphasis. Like all biblical prophets, there are some strong words of warning found in this book. Sin destroys lives. It is dangerous. Phil warns us to flee away. But along with the warnings, there is the wonderful news of God's amazing grace. Phil invites us to trust God's mercy (even if we feel like we have made a mess of many things in life.) There's a truism found on gift-shop plaques and posters that says, "Today is the first day of the rest of your life." As Phil skilfully explains, in Christ Jesus this is not merely a sweet-sounding sentiment, it is 100 per cent true. Because of Jesus, Phil concludes, "Therefore, let me encourage you that today is the day you can start afresh with the Lord. It is never too late to start the process of finishing well."

George Renner, PhD.
Boston, 2018

PREFACE

Whenever one sits down to write a book and follows it through to the end of the publishing process, the questions of worth and motivation must be squarely faced: *Is what I am offering to others of real value?* and *Am I writing this book for others or for myself?*

Of the first question, I will let readers of this book decide its value for themselves. I can, however, answer the second question: it is partly both. And both motivations are so intertwined that is hard to separate them. The life and lessons of Samson struck me vividly as I was reading a Puritan prayer where the writer asked of the Lord that he be kept *"from falling asleep in the lap of Delilah."* This prayer took on greater meaning as I read through the books of 1 and 2 Kings and 1 and 2 Chronicles and was impressed by how many of the good kings started off well but did not finish in the same manner.

I sensed and acknowledged that in my own spiritual journey the danger was real that I too could falter and not finish well: I know the reality as expressed by the Puritan writer:

> Lord, I am sometimes thy enemy; my nature revolts and wanders from thee, Though thou hast renewed me, Yet evil corruptions urge me still to oppose thee . . . There is much unconquered territory in my nature.[1]

Yes, my heart is deceitful and desperately wicked and I have no real understanding of the depths of my depravity.[2] I know my heart is "prone to wander; prone to leave the God I love."[3]

---
1 Arthur Bennett, *The Valley of Vision*, (Edinburgh: The Banner of Truth Trust, 882006), 344-345.
2 Jeremiah 17:9.
3 Robert Robinson, "Come Thou Fount" in *The Hymnal for Worship & Celebration* (Waco, Texas: Word Music, 1986), 2.

And so, I began to think, study, and warn myself to be on guard against the tendency to become complacent in my commitment, to coast in my calling and to cease challenging myself in my walk with the Lord. I want to take to heart the warning of Thomas à Kempis:

> It is vanity to seek after perishing riches and to trust in them. Also it is vanity to hunt after honours and to climb to high degree. It is vanity to follow the desires of the flesh, and to long after that for which you must afterward suffer grievous punishment. It is vanity to wish to live long, and *to be careless to live well.* It is vanity to mind only this present life and not to foresee those things which are to come. It is vanity to set your love on that which speedily passes away, and not to hasten to where everlasting joy abides (emphasis mine).[4]

Therefore, I view this study as an act of public accountability for myself. I desire for the readers to examine my life with the exhortations and encouragements of this book and call me to account if I don't measure up. I want to finish well.

But secondly, I also wrote it for others. Admittedly, a lot of what I discuss is written about the man Samson, for men, and from a man's perspective. In addition, I make many references and applications to those in the pastoral ministry since this has been my focus for most of my life. But there are a lot of lessons and warnings that my sisters and those who are not in the pastoral ministry can apply to their lives as well. We all need prompting to pursue God's will for our lives. We all need to be challenged to go deeper in our walk with God. As Sarah Cunningham said, "The tension between who we are and who

---

4 Thomas à Kempis, *The Imitation of Christ* (Chicago: Moody Press, 1982), 12.

we are striving to become is what keeps us active in the faith."⁵ And I might add, what keeps us seeking to finish well. Thus, I offer this book in the spirit of Hebrews 10:23-24: "Let us hold unswervingly to the hope we profess, for he who promised is faithful. And let us consider how we may spur one another on toward love and good deeds." Ralph G. Turnbull commented on these ideas when he wrote:

> To lose sight of the redemptive mission of Christ, to lose our evangelical passion, to become self-satisfied in our calling – this is the way to lose clean hands, the righteous lips, and the pure heart. It is by the discipline of the struggle within our own hearts that we learn to become helpers of others to whom we would minister. And in humility of spirit we proceed with our work: we plod and still keep the passion fresh. One day we shall be satisfied when we have finished our task.⁶

The observant reader will note the frequent quotes and references from several main sources. The first is Arthur Bennett's collection of Puritan prayers, *The Valley of Vision*. Bennett does not identify specifically the author of the prayers and so when I quote them I indicate generally that is "the Puritan" who has written. The second main source is Oswald Chambers' devotional, *My Utmost for His Highest*. These two have been my close companions during the period of writing this book. I could not help but see in them warnings, confessions, and encouragements that directly related to what I was thinking and learning from the life of Samson. A third major source is *Markings* by Dag Hammarskjöld the second Secretary-General of the United Nations. I first discovered his book in my junior year of high school and have now returned to

---
5 Sarah Cunningham, *Dear Church* (Grand Rapids, Michigan: Zondervan, 2006), 182.
6 Ralph G. Turnbull, *A Minister's Obstacles* (New York: Fleming H. Revell, 1946), 92.

it for inspiration almost fifty years later. *The Imitation of Christ* by Thomas à Kempis has become more meaningful to me now than when I read it as a younger man. In addition, Stephen Farrar's book *Finishing Strong,* which I discovered almost at the end of my writing, has been helpful. We have a different emphasis but much of what we have written supports and complements each other.

This book is not primarily about spiritual disciplines although their practice is vital to finishing well. Living out the disciplines is assumed – and I acknowledge my need to grow in them. Many authors have handled these topics throughout Christian history and their works are readily available.

To Finish Well, You Have to Finish . . .

There is another truth that God has been teaching me through the writing of this book. To finish well, you have to finish! This lesson came to me after I had returned from a three-week training trip in Mozambique. The following day I received news from the Kenyan government entity that the permit for my doctoral dissertation field research had been approved. This was the second of two approvals I had been waiting for since I had applied six months earlier. While I was approved, I learned they had put some unexpected requirements in place that would make doing the research much more difficult. I had been waiting since February to get the two needed permits and this just seemed a bridge too far, a mountain too high to climb.

I swallowed hard, determined to push on, and then the next day after I walked in the door from an early morning mentoring session my wife took a look at me and said, "Are you okay?" And I said, "I am anxious." She came over to me, wrapped her arms around me and started to pray, and I snapped. All the pressure from my ministry, my doctoral work, and mission responsibilities came crashing down and I started to cry, to gasp, and to shake uncontrollably.

It was emotional projectile vomiting. I had no idea it was coming. My body just responded to the stress that I had been living under for the last couple of years as so many things kept piling up and piling on.

To make a long story short, I ended up going to see a counsellor who helped me look at my life and all that I was carrying and dealing with. He said, "I'm not surprised what happened."

It could have been worse, but God was gracious, he allowed me to have this happen, to help me to see that if I am going to finish well, I need to be able to finish. And if I am going to finish well, I need to restructure my life and reorder my priorities and restrict my activities. So, I am in recovery mode as I finish writing this book. "Physician, heal thyself!" (Luke 4:23, KJV). I cannot! Great Physician, heal me!

A book about spirituality is humbling to write as I have become more aware of my own weaknesses and shortcomings. Increasingly, I am aware of how much further I need to travel if I am going to finish well in my own spiritual journey. I believe spiritual maturity is not where we have arrived but the direction we are headed. Therefore, I can only echo what the apostle Paul said in Philippians 3:13-14:

> Brothers and sisters, I do not consider myself yet to have taken hold of it. But one thing I do: Forgetting what is behind and straining toward what is ahead, I press on toward the goal to win the prize for which God has called me heavenward in Christ Jesus.

xxii   Falling Asleep in the Lap of Delilah

Here is a *Man Who Finished Well*!

> Looking to future days to come
> Of my life's work to be done
> What will the results finally tell?
> Will it be
> A faithful man who finished well?
>
> When I struggle with fleshly sin
> Wrestling my pride within –
> And temptations from the pit of hell
> May I be
> By God's grace a man who finished well.
>
> If from cares I see no way out –
> And I'm assailed by darts of doubt –
> Fear causing my heart to swell –
> May I be
> By faith, a man who finishes well.
>
> When my time on earth is done
> When my race is finally run
> What will my epitaph spell?
> May it be
> "Here is a man who finished well!"
>
> When I enter heaven's place
> And I see my Saviour's face
> May I hear my master tell –
> "Faithful son!
> You are a man who finished well!"

Nairobi, July 2018

PROLOGUE

"How did this man come to this place?" she wondered looking intently at the face of the man whose head lay heavily in her lap. Her gaze was hard to read, as it was a mixture of amused amazement that this famous foe was so trusting and so vulnerable. She ran her finger through one of the ringlets of his long hair and noticed that it was flecked with grey. She studied his face and for the first time observed the slight wrinkling of skin. He was not a young man but he was a powerful man still in his prime.

Delilah did not love him, but he fascinated her. She did not hate him either and rather enjoyed the game of wits they had been playing. What *was* the key to the amazing strength of this Israelite man? The truth of this question had been her quest- and now she had it, and with it, a huge reward. She smiled in satisfaction. Soon, it would be all over, and she would win . . . when the barber came.

CHAPTER 1

THE ISSUE OF SPIRITUAL COLDNESS OR "FALLING ASLEEP IN THE LAP OF DELILAH"[7]

I am sitting outside. It is warm. This is significant because our home of stone and concrete construction is quite cold. In fact, it is colder inside the house than outside. We are coming to the end of our winter here in Nairobi. People don't usually think of Africa being cold – but it can be. The winter months of June–August are often grey and overcast – and sometimes damp. The cold creeps into the very structure of our ground floor flat and settles there for the season. But I am sitting outside. The rays of the sun soften the edges of the cold blanket we have been living under and I revel in the warmth.

I wonder how many people are like this? They are cold on the inside while many around them are warm and vibrant. What causes the frigidness of the heart and soul? What causes the natural warmth of a child's sunny disposition to gradually succumb to the numbness of a frost-

---

[7] This title is taken from the following lines from Bennett, 279: "Hast thou sought joys in some creature comfort? Look not below God for happiness; fall not asleep in Delilah's lap."

encrusted inner being? Where does the childish delight of life and wonder go? How do the bright embers of enthusiasm fade? What causes the awe of each new adventure to lose its appeal? And how does a child's openness to God and things spiritual close tightly shut?

Perhaps, it comes as one suffers disappointment, broken promises, unfulfilled dreams, injustice, and abuse. And so, the heart grows cold and an impervious shell of icy-protectiveness forms a frigid zone inside one's soul. Without the reception of love's warmth the inner man becomes an artic wasteland. And yet the person in the pain of spiritual coldness will seek comfort for his or her soul even if it means lowering standards and compromising values.

One day I visited a pastor during the middle of the week and after some conversation we went into the empty sanctuary and knelt at the front of the church to pray. As we prayed, he poured out his heart and urgently pleaded with the Lord, "God, I want your power upon my life." A number of years later he had left his wife, divorced, and married another woman.

How does one come to this place? That question could be asked of many men and women found in compromising positions. Many who have been servants of God with fruitful ministries and have been used by him for the salvation of souls and the building up of the body of Christ have later grown cold and walked away from their calling.

What was the path of failure and faithlessness that led them to turn away from what they had proclaimed to believe? The answer to that question has many parts and can lead in many directions. There are many possible causes contributing to compromise. Some may be common to all; some may be unique to one. But each cause can stand as a warning to others.

Such a warning comes from the life of Samson. He was a man set apart from birth by God for a unique service and the deliverance of his people. He was given great strength. He possessed a keen intellect and used his gifts to fulfil his divine calling that was declared to his parents at the announcement of his birth by the angel of the Lord who said, "he will begin the deliverance of Israel from the hands of the Philistines" (Judges 13:5).

And yet we find him falling asleep in the lap of Delilah, the Philistine woman who fascinated Samson and eventually led him to his downfall. This is a picturesque phrase used of a man who was chosen by God to be the leader of his people. It is also a phrase that should warn all of us about the wiles of the world which would woo God's people into temptation and sin.

Samson seemed to have a soft spot for sensual seductions. Delilah was not the first Philistine woman or prostitute that he had sought out. He had been involved with other women and gotten into other troubles with his enemies. His excuse seems to be that he was seeking an occasion to take action against Israel's oppressors. Yes, they were his adversaries who were subjugating the nation, but using this as a reason to fight against them did not give him the right to disobey God's law and to lower his moral standards. As the old saying goes, "It is never right to do wrong to do right."

Samson was a man of unique physical abilities. He was also very clever and intelligent as seen in the riddle he proposed to his guests at his wedding in Timnah. But more than that, he was uniquely set apart from birth for the ministry of delivering his people. This uniqueness was grounded in the special mode of sanctification found in his God-given status as a Nazirite. The requirements were stated in Numbers 6:1-8:

> The Lord said to Moses, "Speak to the Israelites and say to them: 'If a man or woman wants to make a special vow, a vow of dedication to the Lord as a Nazirite, they must abstain from wine and other fermented drink and must not drink vinegar made from wine or other fermented drink. They must not drink grape juice or eat grapes or raisins. As long as they remain under their Nazirite vow, they must not eat anything that comes from the grapevine, not even the seeds or skins. During the entire period of their Nazirite vow, no razor may be used on their head. They must be holy until the period of their dedication to the Lord is over; they must let their hair grow long. Throughout the period of their dedication to the Lord, the Nazirite must not go near a dead body. Even if their own father or mother or brother or sister dies, they must not make themselves ceremonially unclean on account of them, because the symbol of their dedication to God is on their head. Throughout the period of their dedication, they are consecrated to the Lord.'"

Leon Wood describes the distinctive demands of one who took the Nazirite vow:

> This form of life normally was entered into only for a short time. The person would take the vow of the Nazirite and then drink no form of strong drink, consume nothing made from the product of the vine, refrain from cutting his hair, and make sure never to come near a dead body. At the same

time he was to realize that these outward actions only represented an expected inner dedication of life.[8]

Although Samson enjoyed these special physical, intellectual, and spiritual attributes they seemed to be of little value to him. For a while he disregarded them, disobeyed God's law, and seemed to get away with it. He had an attitude of spiritual exemption that eventually led him to falling asleep in Delilah's lap.

In this study we will look at various dangers that eventually led Samson to Delilah's lap – and which could lead us there as well. This points to the truth that temptations are not new; they are just a variation on a theme as they take different forms from generation to generation and culture to culture. Satan is always intent on bringing to ruin God's servants and destroying their ministry. We would do well to carefully heed the lessons we can learn from the example of Samson's life, for in them we see those issues which will hinder us from finishing well.

As I look at Samson's life and why he ended up falling asleep in Delilah's lap, I believe a primary reason was the need to be comforted. The opposite of comfort is pain. Pain can be little or great. The discomfort can be a matter of degree, but it is pain, in some measure nonetheless. And it seems that by nature, human beings are pain-adverse.

As we look at Samson I believe we see a man who was seeking comfort as an antidote to his pain. This raises the questions, *What was Samson's pain?* and *What internal suffering drove him to seek soothing by lying asleep in Delilah's lap?* As we examine his life we see that there were several possible factors

---
8 Leon Wood, *The Distressing Days of the Judges,* (Grand Rapids, Michigan: Zondervan Publishing House, 1976). p. 307.

that could have caused his pain. To clarify, it would be good to point out that there are different paths of pain. Even when one is seeking to serve and follow the Lord, pain is often part of the experience. We can be squarely in the centre of God's will and living a life of obedience and encounter pain on the path. In addition, not all pain is a result of disobedience. As we look at Samson's life we will see that although much of his pain was a result of disobedience it was not always the case.

The first possible source of pain was the fact of his calling to be a Nazirite from conception. In the circumstances of his birth the angel of the Lord said to his parents, "the boy is to be a Nazirite, set apart to God from birth" (Judges 13:5). He had no choice or say in this matter and this status automatically made him different from everyone else.

These differences included his diet, his dress code, and his decorum (Numbers 6:1-8). He was not to eat or drink any product of the grape vine which included wine, vinegar made from wine, grape juice, grapes, or raisins. His dress code consisted of never shaving his head thus allowing his hair to grow long. His decorum was marked by the fact that he could not go near a dead body. These had to be strictly observed throughout the period of his consecration to the Lord.

Could this have led him to feel isolated from his family and community? Sometimes being different and isolated can cause people to become defensive or defiant. Perhaps, we see some of this in Samson's insistence on acquiring the Philistine girl from Timnah as his wife even with his parents' objections to the match.

Secondly, there was the possible pain of disapproval by his parents over his choice of a wife. When he asked his parents to go through the usual pre-wedding process of obtaining her for him they objected and said, "Isn't there an acceptable woman among your relatives or among all our people? Must you go to the uncircumcised Philistines to get a wife?" (Judges 14:3). Scripture says he was using this situation as a way to do something against the Philistines, but he seemed to genuinely care for this woman. It was likely painful for Samson to have his parents react so negatively against her.

Thirdly, he had the pressure and the expectation that he was the one who would begin to deliver his people from the hand of the oppressing Philistines. That was a huge task and perhaps to Samson it was a painful and overwhelming responsibility. This too, could have led to his anxiety. It is one thing to have a large task but it is another to face it alone and to feel that everything depends solely upon you.

This aloneness was clearly seen in a fourth source of pain, which were repeated betrayals by people close to him. We see this in the duplicity of his bride during their wedding feast. Earlier Samson had killed a lion bare-handed and on the way to the wedding he turns aside to see what happened to the kill and there finds that bees have built a nest in the carcass of the lion. He eats of the honey and shares some with his parents. At the wedding he proposed this riddle to his Philistine friends: "Out of the eater, something to eat; out of the strong, something sweet" (Judges 14:14).

He promised if they guessed his riddle he would give each a new suit of clothing. However, if they could not, then each of them must give him a suit of clothing. They agreed to the proposal and for three days tried to solve it. On the fourth day, the Philistines came to Samson's bride and threatened to burn her and her father's household to death if she did not find out.

She began weeping and told Samson that he hated her until he finally gave in and explained the riddle to her.

She immediately betrayed Samson by sharing the solution with the men who victoriously went to him with the answer. Samson knew they had pressured her and went to a neighbouring town, killed thirty men, took their suits, and upon returning to the feast gave the promised clothing to his guests. In anger, he left his new wife and the guests and went home to Israel. Later, when his rage cooled down he went back down to Timnah to get his wife only to find his father-in-law had betrayed him: "I was so sure you hated her that I gave her to your companion" (Judges 15:1-2).

After two cycles of revenge (Judges 15:3-8) where Samson burned the Philistines' crops and killed a large number of men, the Philistine army came up to capture him. At this time, he was betrayed by his people. In Judges 15:9-13 three thousand men of Judah came down to capture, bind, and turn him over to the Philistines. Samson agreed to be bound, but in a plaintive request asked that his countrymen not kill him. What would have been the alternative if they had not agreed to his request? He would have had to fight and kill his own people. It was a noble but painful response to their betrayal.

Thus Samson tried to numb the pain, tried to find comfort in the presence of a woman from the enemy camp – asleep in the lap of Delilah. How we need to take heed to where we seek to find comfort and solace from our own pain! Delilah's lap represents the deceptive and deceitful claims to comfort and inner peace that the Devil offers us in our times of inner turmoil and anxiety. But it is a false comfort. Delilah's lap does not deliver; it is a deceptive dalliance. To finish well, the man of God must steer clear from the destructive destination of Delilah's lap.

Delilah's lap takes many forms. Some forms seem innocent; from a preoccupation with our digital devices to an obsession with sports or other hobbies. Others are more serious such as the pornographic addiction or the promiscuous affair. But these comforts are false and short-lived and can ultimately undermine and be destructive to our spiritual life. And the desire for comfort can lead us to a spiritual coldness of heart in our relationship with God.

The more serious manifestations are happening with increasingly routine revelations of God's men who have let their guard down and lost their heads in the lap of this deadly lady. One such example is R.C. Sproul Jr., of Ligonier Ministries, who admitted visiting the adultery matchmaking website Ashley Madison. He said he accessed the site "in a moment of weakness, pain, and from an unhealthy curiosity"[9].

The apostle Paul called God "the Father of mercies, and the God of all comfort" (2 Corinthians 1:3, KJV). In him alone is the ultimate source of comfort. Thomas á Kempis wrote of the Lord:

> For if thou wilt truly find delight, and be abundantly comforted of Me, behold in the contempt of all worldly things and in the avoidance of all worthless pleasures shall be thy blessing, and fulness of consolation shall be given thee. And the more thou withdrawest thyself from all solace of creatures, the more sweet and powerful consolations shalt thou find.[10]

As we continue this study we will see other issues in the character and actions of Samson that led him to the comfort of Delilah's

---

9 http://www.christianitytoday.com/gleanings/2015/august/ligonier-suspends-rc-sproul-jr-over-ashley-madison.html. (Accessed September 14, 2015).
10 à. Kempis, The Imitation of Christ (Xist Classics) (p. 43). Ignatius Press. Kindle Edition.

lap. They warn us of the need to be eternally vigilant to guard our hearts with all diligence and to seek our comfort in the arms of God. Thomas á Kempis prayed:

> Draw me and deliver me from every unstable comfort of creatures, for no created thing is able to satisfy my desire and to give me comfort. Join me to Thyself by the inseparable bond of love, for Thou alone art sufficient to him that loveth Thee, and without Thee all things are vain toys.[11]

If we don't find our soul's comfort in the sufficiency of our Lord, we will end up where Samson did. However, there is hope. By God's grace we can finish well. The Puritan pointed the way in this prayer:

> If thou seest in me any wrong thing encouraged, any evil desire cherished, any delight that is not thy delight any habit that grieves thee, any nest of sin in my heart, then . . . Help me to walk the separated life with firm and brave step, and to wrestle successfully against weakness.[12]

---

11 à. Kempis, Kempis, (p. 51).
12 Bennett, 188-189.

Questions for Personal or Group Discussion:

1. If you were to evaluate your spiritual "temperature" honestly would you be hot, lukewarm, or cold? Why would you rate yourself in this way?

2. The author suggests various sources of Samson's pain and pressure that could have led him to the comfort in Delilah's lap: (1) As a Nazirite, he was noticeably different than others; (2) He suffered disapproval from his parents; (3) He was isolated and alone; (4) He suffered several betrayals; (5) He faced high expectations and pressure to be the nation's deliverer. What kinds of pain and pressure have you experienced, or are experiencing now?

3. Where are you looking for comfort? What possible forms of comfort would be your Delilah's lap?

4. Have you denied and buried the pain? Or have you dealt with the pain in a positive way?

CHAPTER 2
THE ISSUE OF COMPROMISE

Originally the word *compromise* meant a mutual promise and to abide by a decision of an arbiter. It is composed of *com*, together, and *promittere*, to promise. Thus, even from the beginning a compromise was a mutual promise between two parties where something substantial was sacrificed. This could have been of differing degrees but essentially the parties involved moved from their original positions.

All compromise is not bad. In certain areas of life, whether in business procedures, use of resources, or desires within a marriage relationship, compromise is the rational and reasonable course of action. But there are times when compromise is wrong and works ruin, especially in the areas of values and principles. In this case a compromise is a change – a shift in belief and attitude which is often followed by behaviour that one once believed was wrong.

Belief begets behaviour. Behaviour besieges belief. If one compromises his or her behaviour, belief has been compromised as well. To be clear, belief and behaviour work in tandem and exert pressure on each other. One can be tempted to change one's behaviour. And if one changes, how does one deal with the internal dissonance when this varies with one's values? One modifies one's belief. This can be seen in Oswald Chamber's descriptive terminology as "spiritual leakage." He wrote:

> If we lose the vision, we alone are responsible, and the way we lose the vision is by spiritual leakage. If we do not run our belief about God into practical issues, it is all up with the vision God has given. The only way to be obedient to the heavenly vision is to give our utmost for God's highest, and this can only be done by continually and resolutely recalling the vision. The test is the sixty seconds of every minute, and the sixty minutes of every hour, not our times [in] prayer and devotional meetings. [13]

A leak in a car's tire allows the air to escape slowly. Little by little. Spiritual leakage is where one changes one's beliefs little by little – one compromises bit by bit. Slowly the spiritual pressure seeps out of one's life and their relationship with the Lord goes flat. I know of a pastor who was adamantly against divorce, but when his child divorced he adjusted his belief to say that it was acceptable. He compromised – he changed his belief to accommodate the child's behaviour.

In another place where he dealt with this topic, Chambers wrote, "Whenever there is spiritual leakage, remedy it immediately. Recognize that something has been coming between you and God, and get it readjusted at once."[14] If we are to finish well the needed readjustment requires repentance of our

---

13 Oswald Chambers, *My Utmost for His Highest* (Uhrichsville, Ohio: Barbour and Company, Inc., n.d.), 51.
14 Chambers, 244-245.

false beliefs and our unfaithful actions that have compromised our relationship with the Lord.

As a pastor I dealt with a man in my church who had been the youth leader and at one time had an effective ministry with the teens. But he left his wife and was living with a young woman who had formerly been in his youth group. When I met with him to ask him to repent and leave this immoral relationship he replied, "No, I believe God wants me to be happy." That is not spiritual leakage. It is a spiritual blowout! Oswald Chambers warned:

> Beware of any belief that makes you self-indulgent or self-gratifying; that belief came from the pit of hell itself, regardless of how beautiful it may sound. Your theology must work itself out, exhibiting itself in your most common everyday relationships . . . You may know all about the doctrine of sanctification, but are you working it out in the everyday issues of your life? Every detail of your life, whether physical, moral, or spiritual, is to be judged and measured by the standard of the atonement by the Cross of Christ.[15]

Spiritual leakage can lead to the possibility or existence of another derivative meaning of *compromise*. According to Webster's dictionary, it can be "a laying open to danger, suspicion, or disrepute; as a *compromise* of one's good name."[16]

I heard the other day of a pastor who had been caught in adultery. I don't know the details – it doesn't matter. What is important is the cost incurred by his compromising behaviour was

---

15 Oswald Chambers. *My Utmost for His Highest*, Updated Edition (Kindle Locations 4294-4300). Discovery House. Kindle Edition.
16 Webster's New Universal Unabridged Dictionary, 2nd ed., s.v. "compromise."

a fractured family, a destroyed congregation, and relationships ruined. This is the legacy of loose living. When it comes to compromise of God's standards, there are no good results. Compromise is corruption. It is corrosion of the Christian's soul, a collapse of the inner life, and a cancer in the body of Christ.

Our personal compromises may be different according to the favourite false god we choose to follow. We all have them – whether it is lust, pleasure, materialism, fame, success, over indulgence, power, or position. We need to realize that a false god is nothing more than a deception from the devil. To worship the false god is an act of compromise and betrayal. The end result is always disaster: "Those who make them will be like them, and so will all who trust in them" (Psalm 135:18). In the end our character becomes opposite of the holiness that God intends for us. Chambers wrote:

> God has only one intended destiny for mankind – holiness. His only goal is to produce saints. God is not some eternal blessing-machine for people to use, and He did not come to save us out of pity – He came to save us because He created us to be holy . . . Never tolerate, because of sympathy for yourself or for others, any practice that is not in keeping with a holy God. Holiness means absolute purity of your walk before God, the words coming from your mouth, and every thought in your mind – placing every detail of your life under the scrutiny of God Himself.[17]

When we come to Samson we see a man caught up by compromise. But to understand this we need to go back to what we discussed earlier in chapter one as what it meant for him to be

---
17 Chambers, Updated Version, Location 4381-4387.

a Nazirite and the required lifestyle his status demanded. These requirements can be summarized as: no eating of the fruit of the vine, no cutting of hair, and no touching a dead body. The whole point of being a Nazirite was to be set apart unto God. "They must be holy until the period of their dedication to the Lord is over . . . Throughout the period of their dedication, they are consecrated to the Lord" (Numbers 6:5, 8).

For Samson, the period of his dedication was his entire life. Since Samson was a set apart as a Nazirite from birth these standards would have been ingrained in his upbringing from his earliest remembrances. How did he fare in keeping these requirements? There are some commentators who clearly feel that he broke all three of these. Obviously, there is no question he broke the requirement when his hair was cut in his interaction with Delilah, but what about the other two?

Those who say he broke the first, regarding the fruit of the vine, point to the wedding feast. They characterize it commonly as a time of drinking wine. However, the text only says, "Samson held a feast, as was customary for young men" (Judges 14:10b). This is not enough evidence to definitively say he broke his vow at this time. He could have abstained while all the others were drinking. That would have taken great strength of character and commitment to his status of being separated unto the Lord. However, this does not seem to fit in with what we know about his character, so it is very possible that he broke his vow on this occasion.

The second part of his vow was not touching a dead body. Here again, opinion is divided whether he broke his vow or not when he scooped honey out of the carcass of the lion. Some say this was a clear violation while others feel that the vow was limited to a dead human body. Be that as it may, there is another law regarding unclean animals which may be applicable here: "Of all the animals that walk on all fours, those that walk on their paws are unclean for you; whoever touches their carcasses will be unclean till evening" (Leviticus 11:27). Therefore, if Samson did not break his vow regarding touching a dead body specifically he still disregarded the law of touching the carcass of an unclean animal and willingly made himself ceremonially unclean.

An interesting point, in light of this, is the statement in Judges 14:9: "But he did not tell them that he had taken the honey from the lion's carcass." Why didn't he tell his parents he had become ceremonially unclean? Was it simply because he wanted to keep hidden the riddle he derived from finding honey in the carcass? Or was it because he knew that his godly father and mother would not approve? We cannot be dogmatic on this point but we must entertain the possibility that he had a guilty conscience at this point.

As we evaluate Samson's life we can see that with his marriage to a Philistine woman and his consorting with a prostitute, he definitely did not fulfil the law's standard of holiness.

Thus as we look at these two requirements we cannot definitively say that he compromised his Nazirite status but it looks like he certainly could have broken the spirit of the law if not the letter. This is a warning to us. Temptation lurks near waiting for the unguarded moment or the intentional movement towards what we know is not right. Ralph G. Turnbull cautioned:

> As long as we are engaged in the work of the ministry we shall be tempted, even as all Christians, and that with subtlety and acuteness. We must live like others and yet live differently. We must move in society, buy and sell, marry and bring up families, just like the rest of men, and at

the same time be thought superior to the world. Our problem will be to live a really unworldly life in an age which will not suffer any marked external separation from the world. This generation will test us through the temptations connected with our private and public lives, and note, not without triumph, how we fall short.[18]

Spiritual leakage leads to spiritual wreckage. That is what we will look at in the next chapters. But we don't have to go down that path. We can be self-aware and turn to our loving Father in repentance asking for his protecting grace to resist compromise as expressed in these excerpts from some Puritan prayers:

> May the dear Son preserve me from this present evil world, So that its smiles never allure, Nor its frowns terrify, Nor its vices defile, Nor its errors delude me . . . And whatsoever I do may it be done in the Saviour's name.[19]

> Destroy, O God, the dark guest within whose hidden presence makes my life a hell. Yet thou hast not left me here without grace; The cross still stands and meets my needs in the deepest straits of the soul.[20]

---

18 Ralph G. Turnbull, *A Minister's Obstacles* (New York: Fleming H. Revell, 1946), 92.
19 Arthur Bennett, *The Valley of Vision* (Edinburgh: The Banner of Truth Trust, 2006), 78-79.
20 Ibid., 127.

Questions for Personal or Group Discussion:

1. The author wrote, "Belief begets behaviour. Behaviour besieges belief. If one compromises one's behaviour, belief has been compromised as well." Can you give an example of one who has changed his belief to adjust to his behaviour?

2. Can you identify times of spiritual leakage or even of spiritual blowout in your life? What steps did you take to repair the leak or the blowout?

3. What are some ways that we can guard against spiritual compromise in our lives?

CHAPTER 3
THE ISSUE OF AUTHENTICITY – RESISTING SECRETIVE AND DECEPTIVE LIVING

Three closely related habits of the soul that can lead us to not finishing well are deception, a lack of integrity, and the keeping of secrets. The adversary of our soul likes to work in the dark – and tempts us to do that as well. However, there are things we should keep confidential. People may confide in us and we should keep those entrusted things a sacred secret. There are many good deeds of kindness and compassion that we may do, which we should keep secret. Jesus said, "When you give to the needy, sound no trumpet before you" (Matthew 6:2, ESV). In addition, there are issues in a relationship between a husband and a wife that should be kept secret.

But the habit of behavioural secrets is a pathway to bondage and ultimately leads to a lack of integrity. There is a certain seduction to keeping secrets of the soul. The little private practices, the "innocent" indulgences, and the "small" sins that we cherish become the winding filaments of Satan's web that strangle our spiritual life strand by strand.

When we turn to Samson's life we see that he enjoyed these little secrets and even used them as playthings in his dealings with the Philistines. In Judges 14:5-9 we read:

> Samson went down to Timnah together with his father and mother. As they approached the vineyards of Timnah, suddenly a young lion came roaring toward him. The Spirit of the Lord came powerfully upon him so that he tore the lion apart with his bare hands as he might have torn a young goat. But he told neither his father nor his mother what he had done. Then he went down and talked with the woman, and he liked her. Some time later, when he went back to marry her, he turned aside to look at the lion's carcass, and in it he saw a swarm of bees and some honey. He scooped out the honey with his hands and ate as he went along. When he rejoined his parents, he gave them some, and they too ate it. But he did not tell them that he had taken the honey from the lion's carcass.

Why did Samson keep the secret from his parents? He knew that his parents, who were committed to keeping the law, were disappointed in his choice of a wife. He knew they would have disapproved of eating honey taken from the unclean carcass of a lion. Thus, to avoid their further censure he just pretended nothing was wrong.

The sin was not in looking at the carcass. It was taking the honey from the skeleton and eating it. But he compounded the problem by not telling his parents about the source of the honey. John Ruskin pointed out the significance of the silent lie:

> The essence of lying is in deception, not in words.
> A lie may be told by silence, by equivocation,

by the accent on a syllable, by glance of the eye attaching a peculiar significance to sentence. All these kinds of lies are worse and baser by many degrees than a lie plainly worded. No form of blinded conscience is so far sunk as that which comforts itself for having deceived because the deception was by gesture or silence instead of utterance.[21]

It is so easy to keep quiet when we feel that our hidden secret sins are "harmless" and there are no victims. However, sin always has consequences that eventually affect others. Often those consequences are things we would never dream could happen. Let's follow the chain of events that came as a result of this secret sin. From the experience, he formed a riddle and set it up as a gambling contest. If his guests could figure out the riddle he would give them each a set of clothes; if they could not, they would each give him a set. His guests forced it out of his bride which resulted in him going to Ashkelon and killing thirty men for their clothes. Burning with anger, he returned to his parents' home and after a time goes back to be with his bride. There he finds his wife had been given to another. In response he destroyed the Philistines' crops and they in turn burned his bride and father-in-law to death. How different would the story have been if he had not sinned and kept the secret about the lion in the first place?

We see that as Samson came near to the end of his life he still treated the truth as a trivial thing. When Delilah pestered and pressured him to disclose the source of his strength he delighted in deceiving her. Ironically, when he should have kept the truth as a secret he divulged it to his ruin. It seems that his sense of moral

---

21 As quoted by Patrick Morley, *The Man in the Mirror* (Grand Rapids, Michigan: Zondervan Publishing House, 1997), 312.

integrity, blurred through his life of unfaithfulness to his calling as a Nazirite, blinded him to the danger he was in as he lay in the lap of Delilah.

This is where a lack of integrity and openness in our life can lead us. We do not have a clear grasp of what is or is not truth nor do we value truth and truthfulness. When this happens, we have given into the moral relativism of our culture. However, that is not the way to God.

The words of David are instructive: "Lord, who may dwell in your sanctuary?" (Psalm 15:1). Two of the many answers deal with the truth and integrity. He said, "He . . . who speaks the truth from his heart (15:2)" and "who keeps his oath even when it hurts (15:4)." To finish well, to live in God's presence, we must be people characterized by truth and integrity. That means no secret deceptive thoughts and hidden deviant behaviours. It means that as we progress to the finish line we become more conformed to Jesus who is the Truth. Patrick Morley wrote:

> No secrets are kept from God; He knows every word we will speak before it is even on our lips. No one else may know, but God knows. The goal of our secret thought life, since it is no secret from God, should be to live a life of personal holiness.[22]

Thus, if we are to finish well we must be men and women of integrity. Stephen Covey agrees: "Eventually, if there isn't deep integrity and fundamental character strength, the challenges of life will cause true motives to surface and human relationship failure will replace short-term success."[23]

---

22 Morley, 324.
23 Stephen R. Covey, *The 7 Habits of Highly Effective People: Restoring the Character Ethic* (New York: Free Press, 2004), 22.

Over the years, I have struggled with truthful living because I was addicted to projecting a perfect image. As a pastor, I could never be wrong or make a mistake. As a husband I was defensive of any criticism because I had to look good. As a father, it affected how I disciplined my children because their behaviour reflected on me. It wasn't until God brought me to Africa that I met another missionary who gently confronted me with my deceptive lifestyle.

I resisted at first, and he told me later that I was the hardest case he had ever encountered. I was a pastor, a missionary, and totally living in a self-deceptive world of trying to project an image of myself that was not spiritually authentic. Others could see it; I could not until God in his grace broke through and began the process of setting me free from protecting my image. I am not totally there. It is my besetting sin, but I am on the right way to authenticity and finishing well. I have learned that we who are on this journey cannot complete it alone. Mark D. Roberts wrote:

> [W]e are to be a countercultural *community* in a world filled with deception, a spiritual family in which we urge one another to grow in the truth. No matter how difficult this kind of growth may be in a hostile world, *we will find the strength to live in complete honesty when we don't try to do it alone* (emphasis mine).[24]

I suspect many have the same problem as I do. So what does it mean to live authentically? Bill Hybels in his book *Honest to God* defines it in this way: "Authenticity means consistency – between words and actions, and between claimed values and actual priorities. Inauthenticity means that we claim to be one thing, then prove to be something else."[25]

---
24 Mark D. Roberts, *Dare to Be True* (Colorado Springs, Colorado: Waterbrook Press, 2003), 81.
25 Bill Hybels, *Honest to God* (Grand Rapids, Michigan: Zondervan Publishing House, 1992), 13.

Simply put: *Authenticity is where what we claim to be matches who we really are.*

One of the best examples of authenticity in the Bible is that of Paul. We see this demonstrated in three main ways. First, Paul **spoke truthfully about himself**. Paul wanted people to know the truth about himself and the things he was going through so he clearly and without exaggeration shared his situation (2 Corinthians 1:8-9a). What was the reason? It was so they could help him by praying as he went through these hard times (1:11).

We also see that when Paul spoke about himself he didn't put on a false front (2 Corinthians 5:11-12). He didn't maintain a false image like the "super apostles" who were causing trouble in Corinth. Their mode of operation was to "take pride in what is seen rather than what is in the heart". They were not authentic, they believed in the image-is-everything type of life-style. The temptation to live for our image is still the same today and leads to inauthentic living.

Paul was also willing to admit his weaknesses (2 Corinthians 11:30; 12:9-10). Paul demonstrated his authenticity by sharing his weaknesses. His motive was not to seek sympathy for himself. Instead, it was to point to the fact that whatever he accomplished in his weakness was only possible through the power of God. I remember reading a book by a pastor of a large Baptist church who said a minister should never admit weakness. He felt that people would not respect him if they knew his flaws. How sad, because it gave the people the wrong idea of who a servant of God was and should be. It was an impossible standard for them to achieve in their own lives and ministry. It was inauthenticity at its worst.

Secondly, not only did Paul speak the truth about himself, but he also **spoke truthfully about others**. Paul spoke authentically about others whether it was positive or negative. We see this in 2 Corinthians 11:13-15 where he described the false apostles as "deceitful workmen, masquerading as apostles of Christ" and in Philippians 3:18-19 where he said "many live as enemies of the cross of Christ . . . their god is their stomach, and their glory is in their shame." Along these lines, Paul's authenticity didn't cause him to flatter. In 1 Thessalonians 2:5 he said, "You know we never used flattery." He simply spoke the truth to others depending upon the need of the situation.

Thirdly, Paul **spoke the truth to others**. He was authentic in his speech; he didn't compromise. We see this in his encounter with Peter in Galatians 2:11-14. Peter stopped eating with the Gentiles and slipped over to the table of the Jews who had come to Antioch. These Judiasers were undermining the integrity of the Gospel by saying that one had to keep the law of Moses in addition to trusting Jesus as their Saviour. This was a dangerous hypocrisy and even led Barnabas and other Jews astray.

Thus, Paul authentically "opposed him to his face" because Peter was being inauthentic. He was clearly in the wrong (Galatians 2:11), hypocritical (2:13), and not acting in line with the truth (2:14).

Paul is a great example of a man who lived authentically and truthfully. If we put his actions in modern terms we would say that he didn't give into the issue of "spin" that is so prevalent in our culture and in our lives today. Spin is a great enemy to authentic and truthful living. But what is it? Mark D. Roberts in his book *Dare to Be True* quoted Bill Press who said:

> There is no good definition of spin. It's easier to say what it's not than what it is. It's not the truth. Neither is it a lie. Spin lies somewhere in between: almost telling the truth, but not quite; bending the

truth to make things look as good – or as bad – as possible; painting things in the best possible – or worst possible – light."[26]

If we give in to spin, we give in to the temptation to live outside of and in opposition to truthfulness. In his chapter on "Spurning Spin" Roberts gave three steps on overcoming sin:[27]

First, make a commitment to avoid deception. This is what Paul told us we should do in Ephesians 4:25: "Therefore each of you must put off falsehood and speak truthfully to his neighbour." Research has shown how common and accepted deception is in our society. Morley cites The Institute of Behavior Motivation, which found that 97 out of 100 people tell lies – and they do it about one thousand times a year.[28] So we can see that this type of commitment goes against the cultural norm in a big way! But this commitment will lead us to authentic living.

Secondly, learn how to recognize deception. As Roberts said: "This isn't as easy as it sounds. Deception, by definition, is deceptive. It hides. It fools us. It is difficult to recognize even in ourselves."[29]

What are some common contexts or settings that tempt us to deceive others? Roberts suggested these:

Perjured Promotion. This could also be called "exaggerated accomplishments". This is when we exaggerate something about our accomplishments, or abilities that make us look better to others than we really are. Do we tend to round numbers up? Do we take more credit than we should – or all the credit for projects

---

26 Roberts, 5.
27 Ibid., 47-50.
28 Morley, 308.
29 Roberts, p. 48.

that we worked on? This can be done on resumes or just in common conversation.

Avoiding Accountability. A simple example is saying, "The glass broke" instead of saying "I broke the glass" when we accidently dropped it on the floor. Additionally, we may engage in blame shifting. We may have had responsibility in something not working out, but we blame it on other team members. Or we are unwilling to admit our failures to others. Whether we have failed to complete a job, or to fulfil a responsibility with excellence we must not make excuses or rationalize why we failed. Instead, if we are going to live truthfully and authentically, we must openly take responsibility and honestly admit why we failed.

Traffic and Tardiness. Roberts points out the lame excuses and other reasons why we are late for meetings. We may point to "poorly" timed phone calls or heavy traffic but in reality these are lame reasons. The biggest reason we offer these excuses is because of embarrassment. I was at a leadership conference in Nairobi where the speaker was talking about the issue of integrity. She asked, "How many of you make an appointment to meet with someone at 8:00 a.m. but then you don't show up until 9:00 a.m.?" She continued, "Then we all use the excuse of the traffic jam. You know there will be a jam. So why don't you plan to leave enough time to make your appointment?"

These are only some of many deceptions and we need to recognize them and others for what they really are. This will come as we begin to turn our hearts into truth monitors and tune them to the wavelength of what is true. Whatever doesn't vibrate with truth is false and therefore we commit ourselves to avoid those words and actions.

Thirdly, Roberts said that we must actively reject deception. Leviticus 19:11 says, "Do not lie. Do not deceive one another." This then would include all spoken and unspoken untruth on our part towards another. Petty or so-called white lies would fall under this command even if we feel we might protect another person's feelings with these. Morely commented:

> Relationships are built on trust. The fragile thread of trust upon which relationships depend upon can easily be broken. The white lie fractures trust in more relationships:
>
>> "I'm glad you called. I was just getting ready to call you."
>>
>> "Let's have lunch sometime."
>>
>> "I'll be praying for you . . . "
>
> *The white lie doesn't hurt anyone*, goes the logic. That's not entirely true, for the teller of the white lie is always a victim, robbing himself of God's blessing.[30]

Rejecting deception means not simply agreeing with others to avoid conflict. This sometimes may be well intentioned, as we want to maintain unity and harmony within our church team, family or with our friends. But this is false harmony built on silent deception. Such areas where we are tempted to this kind of deception would be in discussion about theology, politics, and entertainment, etc. Roberts wrote, "Your commitment to reject deception must be stronger than your fear of disagreeing and risking the loss of another's approval or friendship."[31]

Thus truthfulness in all things is the key to authentic living. There is no authenticity that is based on deception and secrets. Everything must be brought to and lived out in the light

---

30 Morley, 312.
31 Roberts, p. 49.

of God's truth and his truthfulness. There is no other option for the Christian who desires to be conformed to the likeness of Christ. Roberts concluded:

> The path of truthfulness is the narrow path in today's world, by far the road less travelled. But it is the way of God, the way of significance, the way of freedom. If you continue in the Word of Christ, then you will be his genuine disciple. You will know the truth, and the truth will set you free – free to be intimate with God, free from the constraints of your past, free to give yourself away to others in Christ-like service, free to share your life with others, free to speak truthfully so that the light of God might shine into the darkness of this world . . . Let the truth fill your heart, transform your mind, and come alive in your actions. When you feel tempted to twist the truth or leave it behind altogether, remember the sage words of George Herbert: "Dare to be true"[32]

And finish well!

---

[32] Ibid., 179-180.

Questions for Group and Personal Application:

1. What is needed if authenticity is to really take place in our lives?

2. How important is authenticity in the areas of our lives: marriage, family, work, church, and community?

3. Why do Christians find it so hard to be authentic and open with each other and within the Christian community? What is lost if we do not embrace truthfulness and authenticity?

CHAPTER 4
THE ISSUE OF REVENGE

Pastor Okoch was eight years old when he watched Ugandan government soldiers hang his father after they accused him of siding with the notorious Lord's Resistance Army rebels led by Joseph Kony. As he grew older his heart was filled with hatred and bitterness and he looked for ways to get revenge. He became a man filled with anger against the government, the tribes who supported it and President Yoweli Musevni. He resented any and every thing the government did whether good or bad. To him, anyone with a position within the government or stood with its party was a thief and a murderer.

For 27 years hatred seethed and resentment simmered the toxic venom that filled Pastor Okoch's heart. Everything that came out of him was poisonous to his family, community, and congregation. He admitted that he never preached on forgiveness because he did not want to forgive anyone. He even prayed that demons would possess the president and government of Uganda. The desire for revenge ravaged his relationships and his ministry.[33]

---
33 This is a condensed version of the story as told by L. Gregory Jones and Célestin Mussekura, in *Forgiving as We've Been Forgiven* (Downers Grove, Illinois: InterVarsity Press, 2010), 63-64.

This brings us to the question of Samson's personal revenge and the issue of violence. These two are often related. More often than not, when we begin to take revenge we mean to inflict pain and that usually takes the form of some kind of violence. Violence can be physical, but it can also be emotional, psychological, spiritual, economic, or social, to name a few.

It is beyond the scope of this book to delve into all the arguments surrounding non-violence and the accompanying discussion of self-defence. As believers we are not to take revenge. If we follow the teachings of Jesus "we are to turn the other cheek" (Matthew 5:39) and live our lives in a non-violent manner.

In Romans 12:19 we read, "Do not take revenge, my dear friends, but leave room for God's wrath, for it is written: 'It is mine to avenge; I will repay,' says the Lord."

Biblically we can say that God may use the means of force in the exercise of judgement and justice. A term we could use for this is that God is vengeant. *The Oxford English Dictionary* lists *vengeant* as an obsolete word meaning "venging; executing vengeance." I propose we revive the word as we see executing vengeance as a proper response by God to those who act wickedly and are rebellious to his sovereign rule.

Therefore, we see that God can use vengeance; we cannot. It is his job; it is not ours. Miroslav Volf wrote, "Preserving the fundamental difference between God and non-God, the biblical tradition insists that there are things that only God may do. One of them is to use violence."[34]

Obviously, when we speak of not using violence we are speaking in terms of using violence as a means to get personal

---

34 Miroslav Volf, *Exclusion and Embrace* (Nashville, Tennessee: Abingdon Press, 1996), p. 301.

revenge. God commanded Joshua and many others to use violence against the wicked Canaanites. However, in this use of violence they were being used as instruments of God's judgement.[35]

This takes us back to Samson and the revenge that drove his life. Samson had a God-ordained cause and purpose for his life. He was, in a special way, to be wholly devoted to be God, which was to be outwardly expressed by keeping the requirements of his vow.

The heart and motivation of the Nazirite vow was to show a desire for a deepened relationship with God. One wonders as we look at Samson whether this was true in his case. We can be confident that his parents taught him the nature of his call into this special relationship with the Lord. This can be inferred from the interesting exchange between Manoah, Samson's father, and the angel in Judges 13. Manoah prayed, "I beg you to let the man of God you sent to us come again to teach us how to bring up the boy who is to be born (13:8)." When the angel returned, Manoah asked, "What is to be the rule that governs the boy's life and work (13:12)?" And the angel repeated that Samson should be taught the way of the Nazirite.

His parents would also have conveyed to him that he would "take the lead in delivering Israel from the hands of the Philistines" (Judges 13:5). Thus as the Spirit of God stirred him up, he began to embrace the purpose for his life (13:25).

However, we observe that the God-ordained cause of rescuing his people became a self-centred crusade for revenge. The focus was not on serving God by delivering his people but on seeking personal vengeance. Notice how revenge became the

---

[35] Admittedly, this is an involved and complicated subject upon which there is much disagreement and difference of opinion. Such a discussion is beyond the scope and purpose of this study.

stated motivation, like bookends at the beginning and the end of his judgeship. His first blow against the Philistines was fuelled by revenge: "This time I have a right to get even with the Philistines (Judges 15:3)." In Judges 15:7 he stated, "Since you've acted like this, I won't stop until I get my revenge upon you." And then at the end of his life as he stood between the two supporting pillars of his enemies' temple, revenge was still the underlying motivation of the last act of his life as he prayed, "O God, please strengthen me just once more, and let me with one blow get revenge on the Philistines for my two eyes" (Judges 16:28).

What is the warning for us? Why did revenge become the driving force of Samson's life? It was because he substituted his cause in place of his calling. Instead of serving God out of a devoted relationship to him, he served himself. As a result, the cause of God transitioned into the cause of Samson. Rescue was changed to revenge.

What can happen to us when our cause, when our life's work, becomes threatened? If we are not fulfilling that cause as an outward flow of our personal relationship with God, we may very well be tempted to protect it and to take vengeful measures against those who speak or act negatively about our ministry. Oswald Chambers wrote:

> Today we have substituted creedal belief for personal belief, and that is why so many are devoted to causes and so few devoted to Jesus Christ. People do not want to be devoted to Jesus, but only to the cause He started . . . If I am devoted to the cause of humanity only, I will soon be exhausted and come to the place where my love will falter, but if I love Jesus Christ personally and passionately, I can serve humanity though men treat me as a door-mat.[36]

---

36 Chambers, 124.

Samson's creedal belief was the Mosaic Law in the context of his Nazirite vow, but he wasn't passionate about his relationship with God or to live out what the vow represented. Because he wasn't passionate about God, something had to fill that void and he focused on the cause. Again quoting Chambers:

> Naturally, if a man does not hit back, it is because he is coward; but spiritually if a man does not hit back, it is a manifestation of the Son of God in him. When you are insulted, you must not only not resent it, but make it an occasion to exhibit the Son of God . . . To the saint personal insult becomes the occasion of revealing the incredible sweetness of the Lord Jesus . . . It is not your duty . . . to turn the other cheek, but Jesus says if we are His disciples we shall always do these things . . . The disciple realizes that it is his Lord's honour that is at stake in his life, not his own honour.[37]

We may not be violent in our revenge like Samson, but are there other ways we can take revenge? What about holding a grudge? What about cutting off relationships? What about refusing to help a fellow worker with our advice, help, or expertise? What about giving our spouse or friends the silent treatment. What about refusing to cooperate with our group's decision when we feel they have gone in a direction we didn't agree with? These expressions of revenge may not be obvious or visible to most people but the effects can still be damaging.

The damage will not only be done to those we are seeking to revenge, but also to ourselves. Getting revenge can become an obsession. It takes over our thoughts. We are in bondage to that person as he or she controls our emotions whenever we think

---

[37] Ibid., 142-143.

about him or her. We begin to poison ourselves as a "root of bitterness grows up" which will "cause trouble and defile many" (Hebrews 12:15).

What should be the Christian's response to revenge? It is to love our enemies; those that have hurt us maliciously or even unintentionally. And loving our enemies ultimately requires us to forgive them. L. Gregory Jones encapsulated this truth in the light of finishing well:

> The call to love our enemies is difficult; it compels us to face the truth about others and you to struggle to love them. But we are called to do so precisely because the horizon of our life, the call to embody forgiveness, is so much broader than simply the absolution of individual guilt. Set in the context of a *lifelong commitment* to healing the brokenness of our relationships, to learning to live in communion – with God, with one another, and with the whole Creation – the call to love our enemies is a call to faithful witness to the God who refused (and refuses) to abandon humanity as enemies but sought (and seeks) to transform us into friends (emphasis mine).[38]

Jones added:

> Learning to love our enemies is, however, often a counter-cultural practice. Indeed, in many contemporary contexts, where people are habituated into – and in fact rewarded for – hating their enemies and desiring vengeance, Christians must offer a counter-habituation. It must involve learning the habits and practices necessary to

---
38 L. Gregory Jones, *Embodying Forgiveness* (Grand Rapids, Michigan: William B. Eerdmans Publishing Company, 1995), 267.

resist the desire for revenge, and struggling to have those desires transformed by God's Spirit into desires for love.[39]

Remember Pastor Okoch, whose story was told at the beginning of this chapter? Remember how his heart was hardened by hatred and he was bound by his bitterness for 27 years? Is there hope for someone like this? Yes, there is. At a conference on peace and reconciliation, after hearing about how "sincere forgiveness liberates a heart from decay and brings it back to new life with purpose and joyful service to the community,"[40] Pastor Okoch publically confessed his un-forgiveness and desire for revenge and started on the journey of spiritual healing. Jones and Musekura described it this way:

> God in his grace gave Pastor Okoch a new vision and a new heart. Pastor Okoch had realized for the first time in 27 years that he could be set free, his heart and mind renewed . . . He asked for prayers that the God who had renewed his heart would continue to renew his mind so he might bear the fruit of peace and love to all people.[41]

Jones wrote:

> In its broadest context, forgiveness is the means by which God's love moves to reconciliation [not revenge!] in the face of sin. Hence the craft of forgiveness involves the on-going and ever-deepening process of unlearning sin through forgiveness and learning to live in communion with the Triune God, with one another, and with the whole Creation.[42]

---
39 Jones., 277.
40 Jones and Musekura, 62.
41 Ibid., 65-67.
42 Jones, 230.

What are the lessons we see in the lives of Samson and Pastor Okoch? If we are going to finish well, we cannot carry the burden of grudges to the finish line. We must release the weight of vengeance by confessing our bitterness and revengeful thoughts and actions. We can intentionally "learn the habits and practices necessary to resist the desire for revenge." We can learn to forgive and be free – but we can't do it alone. We need the body of Christ surrounding, encouraging, and helping us to finish well!

Questions for Group and Personal Application:

1. Was there a time that you tried to get revenge on someone who mistreated you? What form did that take? Was it physical? Verbal? Holding a grudge? Some other way? What happened? How did it affect your relationship? How did it affect you personally? As you look back do you think it was worth it?

2. Do you have someone who has hurt you that you have never forgiven? Perhaps it is someone in your family, an acquaintance, or a former co-worker. What is keeping you from forgiving them? Why do you think that is?

3. What steps do you feel you should take to forgive and bring about reconciliation in this relationship?

CHAPTER 5: THE ISSUE OF PURITY

> And now, O sons, listen to me,
>> and do not depart from the words of my mouth.
>
> Keep your way far from her,
>> and do not go near the door of her house,
>
> lest you give your honour to others
>> and your years to the merciless,
>
> lest strangers take their fill of your strength,
>> and your labours go to the house of a foreigner,
>
> and at the end of your life you groan,
>> when your flesh and body are consumed,
>
> and you say, "How I hated discipline,
>> and my heart despised reproof!
>
> I did not listen to the voice of my teachers
>> or incline my ear to my instructors.
>
> I am at the brink of utter ruin
>> in the assembled congregation" (Proverbs 5:7-11, ESV).

A study of finishing well, and of the study of the life of Samson, would not be complete if we did not address the sexual issue. Volumes have been written on this subject from all points of view: religious and secular, physical and psychological, social science and biological, abstinence and free. As a species, we are more than fascinated; we are obsessed. G.K. Chesterton described the Roman and Greek worlds as:

> Coloured by dangerous and rapidly deteriorating passions; by natural passions becoming unnatural passions. Thus the effect of treating sex as only one innocent natural thing was that every other innocent natural thing became soaked and sodden with sex."[43]

We could say the same is true of our world as well. Truly, our current culture is soaked and sodden with sex. That should not surprise us. What should surprise is that the same could be said of Christian society and sadly about many pastors in our churches.

I remember many years ago, visiting a Pastor's home, and as coloured TV's were just coming into Kenya, he was excited to show me his new set. He said, "I can't wait. My favourite program is just about to come on." I was curious to see what it was, and when it came on, I was shocked as it was an immoral drama that came from the US! Now if a pastor hasn't learned discernment, what can we expect from our people in the congregation?

We must teach them discernment and the truth of Philippians 4:8: "Finally, brothers and sisters, whatever is true, whatever is noble, whatever is right, whatever is pure, whatever is lovely, whatever is admirable – if anything is excellent or praiseworthy – think about such things."

We must teach ourselves, and our people, to think and question the programmes that are on the air and determine whether we should be putting these things into our minds. When

---

[43] G. K. Chesterton, *St. Francis of Assisi* (Veritatis Splendor Publications, 2013), 17. Kindle.

it comes to all sorts of technology whether it is TV, YouTube, or whatever digital content that comes on the internet, we must practice discernment and encourage and help our people to do the same as well.

Statistics are staggering among pastors in the West who are involved in regularly watching pornography. Of the 1,351 pastors that Rick Warren's website, Pastors.com, surveyed on porn use, 54% said they had viewed Internet pornography within the last year and 30% of those had visited within the last 30 days.[44] What I have discovered in my investigation in other areas, that while we have better researched statistics in the West, human nature and sin is fairly consistent across the world. Therefore, it would not surprise me at all that there are readers of this page who have viewed pornography in the past or who are now involved habitually in the practice.

I believe it is also important to acknowledge the fact that the problem of sexual temptation, and of pornography specifically, is not reserved only for men. Statistics show that the level of women involved with pornography is rising to that of the male population.[45] Thus, what is written in this chapter is applicable to both genders as we all are susceptible to the temptations of the flesh.

As we consider this, we turn to Samson who was living in obscurity with his parents. We have no details of his youth and

---

[44] http://www.expastors.com/how-many-pastors-are-addicted-to-porn-the-stats-are-surprising/. Accessed February 1, 2017.

[45] 1. According to a study published in the *Journal of Adolescent Research*, **about half (49%)** of young adult women agree that viewing pornography is an **acceptable** way of expressing one's sexuality.

2. According to a survey of more than 11,000 college-age women, **more than half (52%)** of young women today are exposed to sexually explicit material **by the age of 14**.

3. According to a study published in the *CyberPsychology and Behavior*, **62%** of women have seen pornography **by the age of 18** (emphasis theirs). (Accessed August 30, 2017) http://www.covenanteyes.com/2013/08/30/women-addicted-to-porn-stats/

growing up to maturity. We are curious how he became aware of his gift of superhuman strength. Again scripture only hints at this: "And the young man grew, and the Lord blessed him. And the Spirit of the Lord began to stir him in Mahanehdan, between Zorah and Eshtaol."

Samson may have felt the stirring of the Lord but he also felt something else stirring up in him. As a young man the attraction to young women began to gain a hold in his life. And so we see in Judges 14:2 that he went down to Timnah and saw one of the daughters of the Philistines there and he said to his parents, "Now get her for me as my wife."

This was a problem for his parents as it was clearly against the law of Moses which did not allow mixed marriages like this one (Exodus 34:15-16; Deuteronomy 7:1-4). His life was to be characterized by a specific range of separation according to his status as a Nazirite. Thus, it would go without saying that he should follow in this broader Mosaic requirement of separation for the Hebrew nation.

However, the attraction of this woman was greater than his desire to be obedient to God's word and thus he wilfully went ahead in pursuit of his desire. This is where we must be so careful to guard our heart because emotions and desires are powerful and are very difficult, if not impossible, to resist if they can take root. The result leads us into disobedience and eventually spiritual darkness. Oswald Chambers writes, "If things are dark to me, then I may be sure there is something I will not do. Intellectual darkness comes through ignorance; spiritual darkness comes because of something I do not intend to obey."[46]

Thomas Cranmer, who was the Archbishop of Canterbury during the reign of Henry VIII may have been thinking of the king's

---
46 Chambers, 151.

behaviour and his succession of six wives in seeking a son when he made this observation: "What the heart loves, the will chooses, and the mind justifies."[47]

King Henry desired a male heir to the throne and when his first wife, Catherine failed to give him a son, he eventually divorced her based on theologically dubious grounds and sought for the Pope's annulment of the marriage of more than twenty years. After the Pope refused, Henry broke from the Roman Catholic Church and set up the Church of England so the Archbishop of Canterbury could do the deed. However, Anne Boleyn, his second wife did not give him a male heir either and she was eventually beheaded on charges of infidelity. From this point on, Henry had four more wives who either died or were executed on various pretexts, as they did not fulfil his desire to perpetuate the Tudor line.

A. F. Pollard's comments on Henry VIII's behaviour could, in many ways, be applied to Samson as well:

> He had an elastic conscience which was always at the beck and call of his desire, and he cared little for principle ... His mind, in spite of its clinging to the outward forms of the old faith, was intensely secular; and he was as devoid of a moral sense as he was of a genuine religious temperament.[48]

It is no wonder that Paul warned Timothy to "flee youthful lusts." They can be a powerful distraction from the divine calling in one's life.

Many years ago a Puritan writer was well aware of the battle of the lust of the eyes and he penned this prayer which

---

47 http://www.goodreads.com/quotes/528599-what-the-heart-loves-the-will-chooses-and-the-mind. Accessed May 7, 2017.
48 A. F., Pollard, *King Henry VIII, An Illustrated Biography* (Kindle Locations 160-163). Shamrock Eden Publishing. Kindle Edition.

ends with God's grace. It echoes the truth of 1 Corinthians 10:13: "No temptation has seized you except what is common to man. And God is faithful; he will not let you be tempted beyond what you can bear. But when you are tempted, he will provide a way out so that you can stand under it." The Puritan wrote:

> O Lord, my every sense, member, faculty, affection, is a snare to me . . . If I behold beauty it is a bait to lust . . . Keep me ever mindful of my natural state, but let me not forget my heavenly title, or the grace that can deal with every sin.[49]

Chesterton stated, "The moment sex ceases to be a servant it becomes a tyrant. There is something dangerous and disproportionate in its place in human nature, for whatever reason; and it does really need a special purification and dedication."[50] But it needs more than special purification and dedication. Our eyes, not just physically, but spiritually, need a different focus – yes even a different object of our gaze. To whom should we longingly look? It is the Lord.

In 2 Corinthians 3:7 and following, Paul tells how the face of Moses was infused with the glory of God when he spoke to God face to face.[51] In the same manner Paul tells us that as we are in God's presence – when we look at God – we too will be transformed by his glory. And in this transformation, there will be freedom. These are words of hope in our battle with the temptation to lust with our eyes:

> Now the Lord is the Spirit, and where the Spirit of the Lord is, there is freedom. And we, who with unveiled faces all reflect the Lord's glory, are being transformed into his likeness with ever-

---
49 Arthur Bennett, *The Valley of Vision*, (Edinburgh: The Banner of Truth Trust, 2006), 132, 133.
50 Chesterton, 17.
51 Numbers 12:8.

increasing glory, which comes from the Lord, who is Spirit (2 Corinthians 3:17-18).

How do we gaze at the glory of the Lord? And what is the glory of the Lord? The glory of the Lord is used in two ways in Scripture. The first is the honour of God. Thus Paul said, "whatever you do, do it all for the glory of God" (1 Corinthians 10:31). When we do things for God's glory, or for the glory of his name, we are doing things that enhance his reputation in the eyes of men. We do things that bring praise to him for his wisdom and his works.

But there is another way that the word *glory* is used. And the best way to explain this usage is to define it. As I have studied God's glory in Scripture, I have defined it as follows: "The glory of God is the visible, tangible expression of the totality of God's attributes."

In the Bible when God's glory is present something is seen such as fire, smoke, or great light (Note: Exodus 16:10; 24:17; 40:34; 2 Chronicles 7:3; Luke 2:9; Acts 7:55; Revelation 21:23). But these were the physical manifestations of all of who God is in the outshining of his attributes.

However, when Moses pleaded with God, "Show me your glory!" in Exodus 33, how did God do it? He hid Moses in a cleft of a rock and passed by him as he proclaimed his attributes!

> Then the Lord came down in the cloud and stood there with him and proclaimed his name, the Lord. And he passed in front of Moses, proclaiming, The Lord, the Lord, the compassionate and gracious God, slow to anger, abounding in love and faithfulness, maintaining love to thousands, and forgiving wickedness, rebellion and sin . . . (Exodus 34:5-7).

God's glory was seen visibly and tangibly in Christ (John 1:14). Philip asked to see the Father and Jesus said, "If you have seen me you have seen the Father" (John 14:9). In other words, God's character and attributes (his glory) are seen in the life and actions of Jesus.

Paul takes this further and says in Ephesians 3:20-21 that glory is not only to be in Christ but also in the church. That means when the world wants to see what God is like in the full expression of his attributes they should see them expressed in the life and ministry of the church! They should be able to look at the church and see the attributes of love, wisdom, longsuffering, grace, goodness, etc. expressed visibly and tangibly. And who is the church? It is you and I and all believers in Jesus Christ. Thus, the question must be asked, "Am I demonstrating the glory of God – his attributes – to the world in my personal life?"

Now we may seem to have gone far afield from the question of sexual purity, but this is one of the keys to overcoming lust and sexual temptation. It is to be transformed by the glory of God as his indwelling expresses his attributes through our changed thoughts and actions. Habakkuk 1:13 says, "Your eyes are too pure to look on evil." As we become more like our heavenly Father, and yield the members of our body to his control, our eyes, too, will become too pure to look on evil.

W. B. J. Martin in his book, *Little Sins, Big Consequences*, wrote, "Temptation begins where the eye lingers lasciviously, tarries and gloats instead of passing by. I may not be responsible for what I see, but I am responsible for the degree of attention I decided to give to it."[52] My accountability partner often asks when I see something that is sexually tempting, "How fast is your reaction time?" meaning, how fast do I look away?

---
52 W.B.J. Martin, *Little Sins, Big Consequences*, (Nashville, Tennessee: Abingdon Press, 1982), 89.

This takes intentional, purposeful effort as we see in this prayer of the Puritan:

> Teach me to believe that if ever I would have any sin subdued I must not only labour to overcome it, but must invite Christ to abide in place of it, and he must become to me more than vile lust had been; that his sweetness, power, [and] life may be there."[53]

Oswald Chambers adds:

> The only thing that safeguards is the Redemption of Jesus Christ. If I will hand myself over to Him, I need never experience the terrible possibilities that are in my heart, Purity is too deep down for me to get to naturally: but when the Holy Spirit comes in, He brings the centre of my personal life the very Spirit that was manifested in the life of Jesus Christ, vis., *Holy Spirit*, which is unsullied purity (emphasis his).[54]

This is the theology behind overcoming sexual temptation. But it is good that we also look at practical ways for dealing with this powerful issue. Therefore, let me spell out three ways to help us overcome.

Take Every Thought Captive to Christ

Oswald Chambers wrote:

> The Spirit of Jesus is put into me by the Atonement, then I have to construct with patience the way of thinking that is exactly in accordance with my Lord. God will not make me think like Jesus. I

---
[53] Bennett, 295.
[54] Chambers, 151.

> have to bring every thought into captivity to the obedience of Christ. "Abide in Me" – in intellectual matters, in money matters, in every one of the matters of human life.[55]

It is in this way that we take captive every lustful thought to make it obedient to Christ.[56] We abide in Christ, we gaze at the Lord's glorious face and he begins to transform our desires and passions into that which pleases him. But this is still too nebulous. How do we do this practically?

First, I believe we must actively fight against and repel the devil's attacks in our thought life. This is an application of James 4:7: "Submit yourselves, then, to God. Resist the devil, and he will flee from you." Truly, the battle for purity is a battle for our minds. Our evil desires, which lead to evil actions begins in our minds. James clearly shows how this process works: "Each person is tempted when they are dragged away by their own evil desire and enticed. Then, after desire has conceived, it gives birth to sin; and sin, when it is full-grown, gives birth to death" (James 1:14-15).

In our modern Christianity we may not be familiar with how we should actively resist our adversary. We may not have an example of how we should do it. Thomas á Kempis models it for us in this way:

> Know thou that thine old enemy altogether striveth to hinder thy pursuit after good, and to deter thee from every godly exercise . . . the keeping of thy own heart, and the steadfast purpose to grow in virtue. He suggesteth to thee many evil thoughts, that he may work in thee

---
55 Chambers, 120-121.
56 2 Corinthians 10:5b.

weariness and terror and so draw thee away from prayer and holy reading . . . Believe him not, nor heed him, though many a time he had laid for thee the snares of deceit. Account it to be from him, when he suggesteth evil and unclean thoughts. Say until him, *"Depart unclean spirit, put on shame, miserable one; horribly unclean art thou, who bringest such things to my ears* [and eyes!]. *Depart from me, detestable deceiver; thou shalt have no part in me; but Jesus shall be with me as a strong warrior, and thou shalt stand confounded. Rather would I die and bear all suffering, than consent unto thee. Hold thy peace and be dumb; I will not hear thee more, though thou plottest more snares against me. The Lord is my light and my salvation: whom then shall I fear? . . . The Lord is my strength and my Redeemer* (emphasis mine).[57]

Secondly, I believe taking captive every thought means that first we must bring that thought to the light. This means we must be willing to confess our lustful actions and the sexual fantasies which we treasure and linger over. These are powerful when kept in secret darkness in our soul. Satan has a powerful foothold in our life. He has a productive tool with which to manipulate us to remain under bondage. He whispers, "What about the shame you would experience, if anyone knew? What about your reputation as a pastor, a church elder, a leader in the community, in your home? All would be ruined. It is better to keep this just between us!" But once they are confessed to God he is "faithful and just and will forgive us our sins and *purify* us from all unrighteousness" (1 John 1:9, emphasis mine). This is where we must start because

---
57 à Kempis, Thomas, *The Imitation of Christ*. Xist Classics, Ignatius Press, Kindle Edition. Location 1060.

in our sexual transgressions we have sinned against him and his divine standard for sexual conduct.

But confession to God is only the beginning – and it may be the easiest step. If we have been involved in pornography, lustful thoughts, or sinful sexual activity we have sinned against others as well. If we are married, we have sinned against our spouse. Unconfessed sexual sin will remain free in our lives to distort and ultimately destroy the relationship with our spouse. Confession to our spouse captures that sin, whatever it may be, and brings it captive to Christ. It is no longer free to wield its destructive power in our life and in our relationship.

If we are single, we still need to confess that sin to a trusted fellow believer. (Men should confess to men and women to women so that even the act of confession does not become an occasion for temptation.) James 5:16 tells us that we should "confess [our] sins to each other and pray for each other *so that [we] may be healed*" (emphasis mine). Bringing our sexual sins to light and having a trusted friend pray for us and hold us accountable begins the process of freeing us from the past and bringing it captive unto obedience of Christ.

The evening after I was working on this section, I had a dream in which I was doing that which I should not be doing. I woke up and tried not to think about those sinful actions, but I was not able to stop! I then cried out to Jesus and the focus of my thoughts shifted away from what was wrong and soon I fell back to sleep no longer haunted by those thoughts. I awoke with the determination that I want to make the names of God and his attributes more of a focus in my walk with him.

If you have never done this before, let me encourage you to take this step to gain freedom from the past. Or perhaps you have confessed the sinful sexual actions of the past. Let me warn you, that sometimes those thoughts will try to break free in your imagination. And as you seek to bring other thoughts captive to Christ, things, images, words, and actions that you have confessed to the Lord and have forgotten for years may start to surface again. This is what has happened to me in the writing of this chapter. So, I had to start thinking about Jesus, and singing songs about Jesus, and calling out to Jesus to help me. And then I also told my wife. She needs to know the battle I am facing so she can pray and encourage me to be pure. It is part of keeping those captive thoughts in Christ's prison so I can be free.

Take Drastic Action

Secondly, dealing with the temptation and terrible attraction of lustful thoughts and activities demands drastic action. Jesus clearly taught this:

> You have heard that it was said, "You shall not commit adultery." But I tell you that anyone who looks at a woman lustfully has already committed adultery with her in his heart. If your right eye causes you to stumble, gouge it out and throw it away. It is better for you to lose one part of your body than for your whole body to be thrown into hell (Matthew 5:27-29).

Of course, Jesus isn't saying that we should literally gouge our eye out. We could gouge both eyes out and still lust with images stored in our mind. This is hyperbole; Jesus exaggerated what we should do to make a point that lust must be dealt with ruthlessly and with radical action on our part. Thomas á Kempis said, "Sometimes, indeed, it is needful to use violence and manfully to strive against the sensual appetite."[58] Steven Kryger wrote:

---

58   à Kempis, Thomas, *The Imitation of Christ*. Kindle Edition. Location 1166.

My friend Dave is a pastor. Men come to him and share their struggle with pornography. He tells them to disconnect the Internet. They tell him they can't – it would make life too hard. Cutting off your hand or foot would also make life hard.[59]

But Jesus reveals what's at stake and the steps that must be taken to avoid – not a smack on the bottom – but the eternal fire. Dave is blunt in his analysis when they refuse to disconnect – they are choosing hell. Are you? One of the greatest dangers for Christians in the West is that we have no idea of the danger we are in.[60]

I heard of one traveling evangelist who would insist that the hotel management would remove the television set from his room before he would stay for the night. The story is told that one hotel refused to do it and so he pulled the cable out of the wall! Truly that is drastic action but showed his commitment to stay pure and to avoid the temptation.

A practical day-to-day action (dare I say that sometimes, moment by moment) is "bouncing your eyes." I discovered it a number of years ago and taught it to my boys as they were growing up. In *Every Man's Battle*, Steve Aterburn and Fred Stoeker outline this practice which has been so helpful to me and my boys that I am sharing it at length.

> Let's . . . consider bouncing. You can win this battle by training your eyes to "bounce" away from sights of pretty women and sensual images.

---

59   Matthew 5:30.
60   Steven Kryger, "Don't Fear ISIS–Fear Your iPhone." Accessed July 5, 2017. http://www.communicatejesus.com/ dont-fear-isis-fear-iphone/

If you "bounce" your eyes" for six weeks, you can win this war.

The problem is that your eyes have always bounced towards the sexual, and you have made no attempt to end this habit. To combat it, you need to build a reflex action by training your eyes to immediately bounce away from the sexual, like the jerk of your hand away from a hot stove.

Let's repeat that, for emphasis: When your eyes bounce toward a woman, they must bounce away *immediately*.

But why must the bounce be immediate? After all, you might argue, a glance isn't the same as lusting.

If we define "lusting" as staring open-mouthed until drool pools at your feet, then a glance isn't the same as lusting. But if we define lusting as any look that creates that little chemical high, that little pop, then we have something a bit more difficult to measure. This chemical high happens more quickly than you realize.

In our experience, drawing the line at "immediate" is clean and easy for the mind to understand. This "line in the sand" seems to work effectively (emphasis theirs).[61]

---

61 Stephen Aterburn and Fred Stoeker, *Everyman's Battle* (Colorado Springs, Colorado: Waterbrook Press, 2000), 125.

Dag Hammarsköld poetically captured this thought in a haiku:
> He lowered his eyes,
> Lest he should see the body
> To lust after it.[62]

So before gouging out your eyes, try bouncing – or lowering – your eyes!

Take a Different Route

A third action is that of taking a different route. This means steering away from the trails of temptation. It means intentionally changing our habits and routines that have worn a smooth and easy path to the pleasures of sin in the hidden rooms of our heart and mind. Solomon warned his son about the adulteress, (and by way of application, we can extend this warning to all sexual temptation) in Proverbs 5:8: "Keep to a path far from her, do not go near the door of her house." And again, in Proverbs 7:25-27: "Do not let your heart turn to her ways or stray into her paths. Many are the victims she has brought down; her slain are a mighty throng, Her house is a highway to the grave, leading down to the chambers of death." As we look at the context, it is likely that these women were well known. Where they lived was no secret. So the best way to avoid the enticement was not to travel the road of temptation that took one near her lodgings.

When I was in Bible College our campus was in centre city Philadelphia. Every once in a while, I would go to the Reading Terminal train station to meet a lady student who was coming back to the college. The closest and most direct route led through a part of town which was not a very good neighbourhood. There were a lot of porn shops, astrologers, and palm readers which lined the streets. On one of my trips to the station I heard

---
62 Hammarsköld, 179.

knocking on a shop window. Turning, I saw a woman waving at me to come in. I quickly hurried on my way but I made a decision never to go down that street again but take a longer and different route to the terminal.

The lesson is clear that if we have fallen into different types of sexual sin and know by what we are tempted and the paths that lead us to those temptations, we need to change our route. If the path is pornographic magazines, we need to be on guard against going to those places where we have usually bought them. If it is the Internet, we need to set up ways to keep us from clicking one click at a time to those sites. It may even be that we need to set up software protections and accountability programs[63] that will help us stay off those sites.

If the path is pornographic movies, either in the cinema or over cable TV, we need to stop our attendance at those movies or block those channels. We might forgo vacations at the beach. These, and other actions, might seem to be extreme to some people, but if we are serious about purity then we will be willing to take these drastic actions and walk these different routes. Thus in this way we begin to take captive every thought to Jesus Christ.

And we should take these actions early at the onset of the temptation. We dare not allow the lure of lust to lodge in our thinking. It will grow in power in our imagination and lead us on a downward path to sinful acts, either in our hearts or bodies or both. The wisdom of Thomas à Kempis counsels:

> We must be watchful, especially in the beginning of the temptation. The enemy is then more easily overcome, if he is not permitted in any wise to

---

[63] For more information and comparison of accountability programmes see Steven Kryger, "Accountability Software – Comparing 5 of the Best Tools," Accessed July 5, 2017. http://www.communicatejesus.com/ accountability-software-comparison/

> enter the door of our hearts, but is resisted without the gate at the first knock . . . First there comes to the mind a bare thought of evil, then a strong imagination thereof, afterward delight, and an evil motion, and then consent. And so little by little our wicked enemy gets complete entrance, because he is not resisted in the beginning. And the longer a man is slow to resist, so much the weaker does he become daily in himself, and the enemy stronger against him.[64]

Isaiah the prophet wrote about God's invitation for his wayward people to return to him. But the people were afraid, as they had seen his judgement and they asked, "Who of us can dwell with the consuming fire? Who of us can dwell with everlasting burning?" (Isaiah 33:14). Isaiah's reply was to list for them a number of righteous ways. Among them was shutting "his eyes against contemplating evil" (33:15). And the result of this righteous living was that their "eyes will see the king in his beauty" (33:17). What captivates the eyes of our hearts and minds? Is it the physical beauty of the human form? Or is it the beauty of the King; of our fairest Lord Jesus? Milton Jones wrote:

> Some of you may be trapped on the Internet looking at sights you can't get away from. Others are lusting after a person you cannot have. Perhaps you have gratified the visual and are now moving on into the physical. How do you get out of it? How do you stop when you have tried over and over again? Saying no will never be enough. If you have failed to stop time after time, you will probably fail again. You don't have enough power or motivation to stop. But once you see God,

---

64 à Kempis, 30.

change is possible. He is not visible on the Web page, in the magazine, in your fantasy, or your afternoon affair. You can't see Him there. You have to leave the lusts behind to see what you are really looking for. And seeing God is enough to do it. It is the only motivation big enough to leave the old stuff behind . . . Once you see that face, you just don't want to look back. No other view satisfies like that one. Seeing God is better than seeing anything else. The lusts that seemed to fill us before never quite satisfy again. They pale in comparison with the glory and radiance of seeing God.[65]

Professor Howard Hendricks of Dallas Theological Seminary studied 246 men in full-time ministry who experienced moral failure within a two-year period. As far as Hendricks could discern, these full-time clergy were born-again followers of Jesus. Though they shared a common salvation, these men also shared a common feat of devastation: they had all, within 24 months of each other, been involved in an adulterous relationship. After interviewing each man, Hendricks compiled four common characteristics of their lives:

1. None of the men were involved in any kind of real personal accountability.

2. Each of the men had all but ceased having a daily time of personal prayer, Bible reading, and worship.

3. More than 80 per cent of the men became sexually involved with the other woman after spending significant time with her, often in counselling situations.

---

[65] Milton Lewis, *Sundays with Scottie* (Siloam Springs, Arkansas: Leafwood Publishers, 2003), 116-117.

4. Without exception, each of the 246 had been convinced that sort of fall "would never happen to me."[66]

Just like these men, Samson was carried away by his lust and therefore forfeited his ministry and eventually his life as a result. His example stands as a serious warning to us all if we seek to find comfort in the pleasures of the flesh and sinful sexual behaviour.

Here is a prayer by the Puritan that can help us to have the right attitude in the battle for purity and to finish well in this area:

> O Lover of Thy people . . . I desire to conquer self in every respect, to overcome the body with its affections and lusts, to keep under my flesh, to guard my manhood from all grosser sins, to check the refined power of my natural mind, to live entirely to thy glory . . .[67]

---

66 Garrett Kell, "The Pattern Among Fallen Pastors". Accessed October 26, 2017. https://www.thegospelcoalition.org/article/the-pattern-among-fallen-pastors
67 Bennett, 223.

Questions for Group and Personal Application:

1. Samson sought comfort in the arms of prostitutes and in the lap of Delilah. Where are you tempted to seek comfort when you are hurt, weary, or discouraged?

2. What are the paths that you may be tempted to follow which would lead you to sexual temptation and impurity? What strategies do you employ to avoid running down those trails of temptation?

3. Have you ever said to yourself that failing sexually would never happen to you? What attitude does this show in a person's heart if he or she says this? What should be the attitude of one's heart in the area of sexual temptation?

4. One of the strategies given in this chapter is to change our focus from the temptation by bringing our thoughts into captivity to Jesus. What practical ways do you use in your own life to focus on the Lord and his glory in order to shift your focus from sexual temptation?

CHAPTER 6

THE ISSUE OF ISOLATION

When we were in our late twenties, my younger brother, Mark, and I decided to run a marathon. However, living in different states, we entered separate races. We both ran good times, with his being several minutes faster than mine. I believe there was a good reason for this. I ran the last few miles alone – and at an ever-slower pace. He had friends who came and paced him in. I had no support. I had no encouragement. Mark, however, was surrounded by people who kept urging him on by their words and presence. He finished well. Myself? Not as well as I could have.

One of the truths about Samson that strikes me is the quality of isolation or "aloneness" that seems to fill his life and ministry. It may be an argument from silence but there is no record of others coming alongside him in his battles and efforts to fulfil his calling to begin the liberation of Israel from the Philistines. He led no armies as Gideon. He had no companion like Jonathan's armour-bearer who followed him into battle with the words, "Go ahead: I am with you heart and soul."[68] When Samson's own people wanted to

---

[68] 1 Samuel 14:7.

turn him over to the Philistines, which would have meant his death, he had no one to stand beside him as Jonathan stood with David. Jonathan found his friend, fleeing for his life in the desert, and encouraged David to "find strength in God."[69] No, Samson is an example of the truths that "it is not good for man to be alone" (Genesis 2:18) and "two are better than one, because they have a good return for their work" (Ecclesiastes 4:9).

After Samson's broken marriage to the Philistine woman from Timnah it seems he did not try marriage again. His ministry of delivering the nation was all a single-handed effort, as he did not raise an army or even a band of men to help him. Thus, he faced life and ministry alone. One wonders if this aloneness and loneliness led him into the arms of the prostitute in Gaza and the mercenary minded Delilah.

We were designed as social beings and it is evident that the normal methodology of Jesus and Paul was to work in and with teams. In fact, Paul's desire was to surround himself with others when he was facing life and ministry. With only Luke at his side he instructs Timothy to come to him quickly (2 Timothy 4:9), and to get Mark on his way (4:11). In this fellowship of friends Paul was supported in his desire to serve God and ultimately finish well.

However, there are times when God calls some of his servants to work entirely alone. Elijah is one of the outstanding examples of this, and although he had a servant, it seems that he derived very little spiritual or emotional support from the man. And thus, as Elijah fled from Jezebel and came to Mt. Horeb, he poured out his complaint to God: "I am the only one left" (1 Kings 19:14). And in his aloneness God met him, comforted him,

---
69 1 Samuel 23:16.

and commissioned him for future ministry. But Elijah's solitary ministry is more the exception than the rule.

One version of a popular proverb says, "If you want to travel fast, go alone; if you want to travel far take someone with you."[70] Thus, if you want to finish well – going far – consider who are those that are like-minded who can support, help, and encourage you in the ministry to which you have been called. I know for me, feeling alone or isolated from others in carrying out my ministry are the times when I am the most discouraged and even want to quit or give up. If you don't have anyone, ask God to show you who can enter into the work with you.

Another part of being alone is the lack of accountability. I believe this is one of the reasons people often do not finish well. There can be many reasons for little or no accountability. We may have no one we trust. For some men it is difficult to develop a close relationship with another man. We may not have teachable spirits. Others find it difficult, if not impossible to be vulnerable. And the besetting sin of pride makes us unwilling to humble ourselves in the presence of another person and admit that we have weaknesses. If this is true of us we are in danger of not finishing well. As Patrick Morley wrote:

> Some men have spectacular failures where in a moment of passion they abruptly burst into flames, crash, and burn. But the more common way men get into trouble evolves from hundreds of tiny decisions – decisions which go undetected that slowly like water tapping on a rock, wear down a man's character. Not blatantly or precipitously,

---

70 This is popularly referenced as an African Proverb, however Jia Tolentino tried to trace its origin and came up with no definitive result in "On the Origin of Certain Quotable 'African Proverbs'": (Accessed July 30, 2017). http://jezebel.com/on-the-origin-of-certain-quotable-african-proverbs-1766664089.

> but subtly, over time, we get caught in a web of cutting corners and compromise, self-deceit and wrong thinking, which goes unchallenged by anyone in our lives.[71]

There seems to be no one besides his parents who tried to speak into his life when Samson wanted to marry the Philistine woman from Timnah. And that was input Samson ignored. Most likely, at the end of his life his parents were dead and there was no one in his life to restrain him. Some of the kings of Israel had prophets who tried to hold them accountable. David had Nathan, Ahab had Elijah, Zedekiah had Jeremiah, but Samson was alone – and unaccountable – and he did not finish well. Steve Farrar wrote:

> The hot word right now in Christian circles is "accountability". And it ought to be . . . One of the primary ways that the enemy keeps a guy from finishing strong is isolation. Instead of being close to anyone, you become distant. Instead of being gut-level honest, you begin to shade the truth. And instead of following Christ you begin to *act* like you are following Christ. That's what happens when a guy gets isolated and tries to go one-on-one with Satan (emphasis his).[72]

And guess who loses that battle? It sounds a lot like Samson who lived and served in isolation. But it also sounds like a lot of men and women who refuse to enter into an accountability relationship.

In simple terms, what does it mean to be accountable – and how can that help us finish well? Morley gives a helpful

---

71 Patrick Morley, *The Man in the Mirror* (Grand Rapids, Michigan: Zondervan Publishing House, 1997), 336.
72 Steve Farrar, *Finishing Strong* (Colorado Springs, Colorado: Multnomah Books, 1995), 67.

definition: "To be regularly answerable for each key area of our lives to qualified people."[73] How can we simplify this so that it becomes something meaningful and manageable in our lives? There are three basic things we can do.

Select a time. Good intentions will not lead to accountability. Along with your partner, accountability is something that you must intentionally schedule. This is usually one of the last things I do with the men I meet with. Our meetings are a priority for us and so we select the next time for our sharing before we part. How often you should meet depends on factors such as your family and work commitments or even distance from each other. Some suggest weekly meetings for continuity purposes, but I have found that bi-weekly and monthly meetings have worked as well. Much depends on the commitment level you and your partner have to be accountable.

Select someone. Morely's definition talks about a qualified person. This must be a person who you trust, who is godly, discerning, and wise. The accountability partner should also be someone of your own gender to avoid temptation, as this kind of deep personal sharing can lead to emotional attachment and even physical engagement. The accountability partner can be older but should be someone who is open and transparent in his or her own life and willing to be held accountable as well. Thus, this is different than coaching or mentoring as accountability functions better when there is more of a peer-oriented discipline.

Select accountability areas. In some sense, we should desire to be held accountable in every area of our life. However, some areas may be more difficult for us than others. Morely suggests certain broad areas we should consider such as moral,

---

73 Ibid., 337.

spiritual, financial, and relational.[74] But within these areas we need to be more specific – and we may not have as much difficulty in some of these as others. Because our time may be limited with our partner, and for the sake of effectiveness, it may be good to choose a few areas to concentrate on at a time. This is especially true when dealing with character or behavioural issues. Otherwise, trying to work on too many areas can be overwhelming and lead to frustration or even giving up. However, reporting on a few specific items on your accountability agenda, every meeting is more doable and less daunting. Other areas of accountability may only be occasional or for a season of life, such as short-term goals which you would report on until accomplished. You can always add other areas as you go along.

When we enter into an accountability relationship we are fulfilling the exhortation of the writer of Hebrews to "see to it brothers, that none of you has a sinful, unbelieving heart that turns away from the living God. But encourage one another daily, as long as it is called Today, so that none of you may be hardened by sins deceitfulness" (Hebrews 3:12-13). And in so doing we will be helping and encouraging each other to finish well.

---

74 Ibid., 343.

Questions for Group and Personal Application:

1. Have there been times in your life and ministry that you have been – or felt that you have been – all alone? How did that affect you emotionally and spiritually? What was the reason for your isolation? If you are all alone now, what steps could you take to find the support and encouragement that you need to be spiritually and emotionally strong?

2. The other issue raised regarding isolation is that of accountability. What is the danger to us if we avoid accountability? What is the positive value of accountability?

3. Are you satisfied with the level of accountability in your life at the present? What steps could you take to improve accountability in your life?

CHAPTER 7

THE LOSS OF SPIRITUAL POWER

> You cannot play with the animal in you without becoming wholly animal, play with falsehood without forfeiting your right to truth, play with cruelty without losing your sensitivity of mind. He who wants to keep his garden tidy doesn't reserve a plot for weeds.[75]

Surely, Samson did not keep his garden tidy. His inner life was a plot for the weeds of sin to grow. And eventually he reaped a harvest of thorns and thistles in his life. We see this after he had been dallying with Delilah and finally divulged the secret of his strength to her. She coaxed him to fall asleep in her lap and then called in the barber who shaved his hair. When she sounded the alarm that the Philistines had come, he aroused himself and thought he would go out and foil them as he had done before. But "he knew not that the Lord had departed from him" (Judges 16:20).

---

75 Dag Hammarsköld, Leif Sjöberg and W. H. Auden, trans., *Markings* (New York: Alfred A. Knoph, 1964), 15.

These are some of the saddest words in Scripture. A man who was called, gifted, and had been used by God was now totally unaware of his spiritual condition. Oswald Chambers wrote: "Are you drawing your life from any other source than God Himself? *If you are depending upon anything but Him, you will never know when He is gone*" (emphasis mine).[76]

Herbert Lockyer illustrated the results of Samson's loss of awareness of God's presence in his life as detailed in Judges and showed it to be a disastrous downward spiral:

Self-confidence: "I will go out" (16:20).

Self-ignorance: "He wist [knew] not" (16:20).

Self-weakness: "The Philistines laid hold on him" (16:21).

Self-darkness: "They put out his eyes" (16:21).

Self-degradation: "They brought him *down* to Gaza" (emphasis his) (16:21).

Self-bondage: "They bound him with fetters" (16:21).

Self-drudgery: "He did grind in the prison-house" (16:21).

Self-humiliation: "Call for Samson, that he may make us sport" (16:25, 27).[77]

To these we could add: Self-destruction" (16:30) as Samson took his own life when he collapsed the Philistine temple.

Richard Baxter, in his classic book on ministry, *The Reformed Pastor* warned:

Take heed therefore, brethren, for the enemy hath a special eye upon you. You shall have his most

---

[76] Oswald Chambers, *My Utmost for His Highest*, 14.
[77] Herbert Lockyer, *All the Men of the Bible* (Grand Rapids, Michigan: Zondervan Publishing House, 1958), 292.

The Loss of Spiritual Power

> subtle insinuations, and incessant solicitations, and violent assaults. As wise and learned as you are, take heed to yourselves lest he outwit you. The devil is a greater scholar than you, and a nimbler disputant; he can transform himself into an angel of light to deceive . . . and cheat you of your faith or innocence, and *you shall not know that you have lost it*: nay, he will make you believe it is multiplied or increased, when it is lost . . . Oh what a conquest will he think he hath got, if he can make a minister lazy and unfaithful – if he can tempt a minister into covetousness or scandal . . . O do not so far gratify Satan – do not afford him so much sport: suffer him not to use you as the Philistines did Samson – first to deprive you of your strength, and then to put out your eyes, and so to make you the matter of his triumph and derision (emphasis mine).[78]

Why did Samson lose his spiritual power? Was it not because he became self-centred and self-indulgent? He focused on his own needs and desires and misused the gift he was given for his own self-protection instead of for his God-given mission.

While in prison on a charge of sodomy, Oscar Wilde wrote these telling words about his own life that so easily could have been written by Samson:

> The gods have given me almost everything, but I let myself be lured into long spells of senseless and sensual ease. Tired of being on the heights, I deliberately went to the depths in search of a new sensation . . . I took pleasure where it pleased me, and passed on. And I forgot that every little

---
78 Richard Baxter, *The Reformed Pastor* (New York: American Tract Society, n.d.), 118-119.

action of the common day makes or unmakes character. And that therefore, what one has done in the secret chamber, one has someday to cry aloud from the housetop. I ceased to be lord over myself. I was no longer the captain of my soul, *and I did not know it.* I allowed pleasure to dominate me, and I ended in horrible disgrace (emphasis mine).[79]

When the final crisis came for Samson, he was so self-absorbed in his pleasure that he did not even realize spiritual disaster had come upon him. He had been lulled to sleep in the lap of Delilah. When she sounded the alarm that the Philistines were upon him, instead of trusting in God to save him, he went out to save himself, only to find that he could not. Thus, we can see the truth of the Puritan's prayer:

> Teach me that Christ cannot be the way if I am the end, That he cannot be Redeemer if I am my own saviour.[80]

So what is the lesson for us if we are to finish well? We cannot rely on our own strength. Each day, as we live, serve, and fight the good fight we must be totally dependent upon the enabling power of Almighty God through the indwelling of the Holy Spirit. As the hymn writer said:

> Stand up, stand up for Jesus,
>
> Strand in his strength alone;
>
> The arm of flesh will fail you –
>
> *Ye dare not trust your own;*

---

[79] As quoted by Steve Farrar, *Finishing Strong* (Colorado Springs, Colorado: Multnomah Books, 1995), 153.

[80] Arthur Bennett, *The Valley of Vision*. (Edinburgh: The Banner of Truth Trust, 2006). p. 309.

Put on the gospel armour,
Each piece put on with prayer;
Where duty calls, or danger,
Be never wanting[81] there.[82] (emphasis mine)

Questions for Group and Personal Application:

1. Samson misused the gift he was given for his own self-protection instead of for his God-given mission. Can you think of an example of how one might be tempted to use their God-given gifts for their own personal benefit instead of for the ministry entrusted to them? Can you think of an example in your own life?

2. The author traces the loss of spiritual power to self-centeredness and self-indulgence. What are areas that you tend to be self-centred or self-indulgent? What safeguards do you have in place or need to put in place so that they won't sap your spiritual power?

---

81 "lacking".
82 George Duffield, Jr., "Stand Up, Stand Up for Jesus" in *The Hymnal for Worship & Celebration* (Waco, Texas: Word Music, 1986), 477.

CHAPTER 8

THE ISSUE OF CONCENTRATION

We have been exploring reasons why Samson failed as a leader. What finally led to him being imprisoned, having his eyes gouged out, and being condemned to a life of ridicule and slavery grinding grain? One reason is what Oswald Chambers called a relapse of concentration. It is a point in our life when our focus turns from a careful cultivation of our inner life to other interests or activities. It comes when our relationship to God begins to fade and our commitment to obey his will begins to lose its importance.

Chambers described it in this way: "Beware of the thing of which you say – 'Oh, that does not matter much.' The fact that it does not matter much to you may mean that it matters a very great deal to God. Nothing is a light thing to God."[83] Instead, we need to pray as the Puritan did: "Let me never undervalue or neglect any part of thy revealed will."[84]

As we look at Samson, he undervalued his Nazirite vow and the revealed will of God in

---

83 Chambers, 76.
84 Arthur Bennett, *The Valley of Vision* (Edinburgh: The Banner of Truth Trust, 2006), 255.

his calling to begin to rescue the nation from the oppression of the Philistines. The secret of having not cut his hair – and what it represented – no longer mattered much to him. It became a light thing to him as he playfully matched wits with Delilah by giving her fanciful notions of the source of his strength. It became a toy, a bauble, instead of a sacred gift from God.

If ever we take for granted, or as a light thing, the stewardship of the spiritual gifts God entrusts to us for spreading the Gospel and the edification of the body of Christ, we have had a lapse of concentration. We are in grave danger of losing the spiritual power God has given to us. Samson thought it a light thing. He thought it only as play and so can we! But the enemy is patiently waiting for the right opportunity to spring upon us when we have been lulled to sleep in Delilah's lap.

Samson's concentration waned because he became emotionally worn down. Daily Delilah pestered him for the secret of his strength as she pleaded, cajoled, and accused Samson of not loving her. Judges 16:15-18 tells the story:

> Then she said to him, "How can you say, 'I love you,' when you won't confide in me? This is the third time you have made a fool of me and haven't told me the secret of your great strength." With such nagging she prodded him day after day until he was sick to death of it.

Dag Hammarskjöld warned: "Never 'for the sake of peace and quiet.' deny your own experience or convictions."[85] We can be emotionally attacked and pressured by those around us who desire we do something wrong and against our standards. They can be relentless in their assaults. They may accuse us of dishonesty, disloyalty, and a denial of our friendship. And it is

---
85 Dag Hammarskjöld, 84

in that moment of weakness as we are ready to cave in to their demands and desires that our concentration on God's will and standards becomes distracted by the emotion of the moment.

So we see that Samson's playing lightly with holy things lulled him into a sense of complacency and a lack of spiritual concentration that eventually led to his downfall. Therefore, if we are going to finish well, we must esteem highly the gifts and calling of God. And we must concentrate well on our calling as children of God and what that means for holy and sober living.

The Puritan writer framed what happened to Samson and what can happen to us when he prayed:

> Thou dost not play in convincing me of sin, Satan did not play in tempting me to it, I do not play when I sink in deep mire, For sin is no game, no toy, no bauble; Let me never forget that the heinousness of sin lies not so much in the nature of the sin committed, as in the greatness of the Person sinned against.[86]

This lapse of concentration did not happen all at once. It was a result that came through a pattern of living he practiced over a lifetime. If we could put it in another way, it was a result of drifting away from the truth. He no longer concentrated on his calling and his position of being set apart by God.

This means that we must intentionally call ourselves back to introspection upon our own inner-life. We must concentrate on what really matters. And we must make what matters to God matter to us. I must admit that I don't like personal introspection. I much prefer the way of excuse and rationalization. I favour the way of thinking that my sins are only light things and that in the

---
86 Bennet., 143.

main, "I know I am right with God." Introspection is often too painful for me so I choose to relapse my concentration on my spiritual state. Why is this? Because introspection about my inner being will lead me to areas of my weakness. I know that I will need to change – usually a costly and painful process.

Perhaps, never in the history of mankind has it been easier to shift our concentration away from things that matter to things that have little or no importance at all. With the rise of the manifold forms of media, the internet, and entertainment all clamouring for our attention, the ability to concentrate on what matters most to God – and thus to ourselves – becomes increasingly difficult.

"In quietness and trust is your strength," Isaiah said (Isaiah 30:15), but there is no quiet for the modern pilgrim. There is none unless we consciously choose to carve out times to care for our soul and to concentrate on the still small voice of God's Spirit whispering and wooing us to focus on that which really matters. And yet, in the busy pressure of our lives we feel that we do not have the time, or that we cannot take the time, to hide ourselves away from all the distractions and the immediacy of life's interruptions. We feel there is no time to wait and say, "Speak, Lord for your servant is listening" and to concentrate on hearing his tender, loving, convicting, caring voice as he works his healing wonder in our wounded hearts. Thus in the spirit of introspection Chambers asked:

> Are there things in connection with your bodily life, your intellectual life, upon which you are not concentrating at all? You are all right in the main but you are slipshod; there is a relapse on the line of concentration. *You no more need a holiday from spiritual concentration than your heart needs*

a holiday from beating. You cannot have a moral holiday and remain moral, nor can you have a spiritual holiday and remain spiritual. God wants you to be entirely His, and this means that you have to watch to keep yourself fit. It takes a tremendous amount of time (emphasis mine).[87]

Concentration takes self-discipline as well. When we look at the life of Samson, he seems to lack discipline in his life. What we know of Samson's life in Scripture is a man who is reacting to provocation and indulging in an unregulated life-style. Oswald Chambers said, "we put things down to the devil instead of our own undisciplined natures."[88] Blaming the devil instead of exercising self-control is a convenient way of excusing our behaviour and soothing our conscience. But it does no good in developing Christ-like character and godly behaviour.

Concentration Restored

As we look at the concluding chapter of Samson's life we see that he finally returns to the Lord and acknowledges the source of his power. This is when he prayed for strength so that he could destroy the Philistine temple. His concentration is restored. We see that he has learned the lesson that God was trying to teach him. He realized that without God's presence and power in his life he was totally helpless and could do nothing. But the process was painful as he was humiliated, abused, and enslaved. The price was high as it cost him his life.

Oswald Chambers commented, "How much longer are some of us going to keep God trying to teach us one thing? He never loses patience. You say – 'I know I am right with God'; but

---

87 Chambers, 76-77.
88 Ibid. 102.

still . . . there is something over which you have not obeyed."[89] God never loses patience but if we persist in our own way, the path of our life will be strewn with the wreckage of our wasted potential.

Turning our concentration back to God and responding to his gracious invitation into a deep and full relationship with him is the path to finishing well and to use our God-given gifts and abilities to the maximum.

Here is a prayer for all of our hearts from the Puritan writer so that we might not waste our potential but finish well:

> Deliver me from attachment to things unclean, from wrong associations, from the predominance of evil passions, from the sugar of sin as well as its gall, that with self-loathing, deep contrition, earnest heart searching, I may come to thee, cast myself on thee, trust in thee, cry to thee, be delivered by thee.[90]

---

89 Chambers, 76.
90 Bennet, 146-147.

Questions for Group and Personal Application:

1. Oswald Chambers wrote, "Nothing is a light thing to God." What thing or areas of life do you, or the Christian public at large, tend to take lightly?

2. Dag Hammarskjöld warned us, "Never 'for the sake of peace and quiet' deny your own experience or convictions." Have you ever been tempted just to give in and deny your convictions because family or friends have continually pressured you? What was that like for you? What have you done to deal with this lapse of concentration in your life?

CHAPTER 9: THE ISSUE OF DRIFT

When I was a boy our family would take a vacation on a small lake in the Finger Lake region of New York. One of the things that I enjoyed doing was taking a row boat out into the middle of the lake and then pulling in the oars and just laying back in the sun and enjoying the subtle rocking as the waves lapped up against the side of the boat. After a while of "sitting still" I was always amazed at how far I had drifted from my original place. I had done nothing to move the boat but the current had carried me along.

This is how life can be if we are not intentional about where we want to go and how we are spending our life. Making progress means effort on our part. It means that we must have a purpose to pursue, a goal to achieve. As we discussed in the previous chapter finishing well requires concentration. Without it we can begin to drift.

Drifting is a danger all of us face after we have accomplished objectives and achieved some measures of success. We can begin to relax and stop growing and learning. Thomas à Kempis wrote, "If you think that you know many things and understand them well, know also that there are far more things which you do not know." Instead of drifting through life we should be life-long learners.[91]

J. Robert Clinton calls this relaxing and lack of continued growth and learning "plateauing." It can easily turn into the kind of drifting we are describing. He explained it in this way: "Leaders who plateau early reveal a common pattern. They learn new skills until they can operate comfortably with them, but then they fail to seek new skills deliberately and habitually. They coast on prior experience."[92] Later he added:

> All leaders have the capacity to influence. God wants to develop that capacity over a lifetime. Leaders often reach a point . . . in which their development seems arrested. This is the plateau barrier. They may be content to continue with their ministry as is, without discerning the need to develop further.[93]

As I study the life of Samson, I don't clearly see the issue of drift in his life, although it seems to be there when we see how his early days are described: "The woman gave birth to a boy and named him Samson. He grew and the Lord blessed him, and the Spirit of the Lord began to stir him" (Judges 13:24-25). There was a real spiritual connection between Samson and the Lord but something happened. We don't see any sudden act of apostasy or turning away, but as we have looked earlier there were choices that he made that could easily be the result of drifting away and which undermined his calling and his separation to the Lord.

Because this is such a key issue in hindering us from finishing well, I want to look at the life of another judge that clearly

---
91 à Kempis, 14.
92 J. Robert Clinton, *The Making of a Leader* (Colorado Springs, Colorado: NavPress, 1988), 89.
93 Ibid., 114-115.

illustrates the process of spiritual drift. This is seen in the life of Gideon, who started well and through faith was used mightily of God to deliver the Israelite nation. However, after the victories were won he drifted, and at the end of his life we see that he did not finish well.[94]

After Israel's enemies are defeated, the people came to Gideon, and said, "Rule over us – you, your son and your grandson – because you have saved us out of the hand of Midian" (Judges 8:22). This was an amazing offer of a dynasty to a man who only a short time earlier was a nobody and who said my "clan is the weakest in Manasseh and I am the least in my family" (6:15).

The temptation to take credit and assume power was very real and yet Gideon choose to do the right thing by turning down the offer by saying, "The Lord will rule over you." In so doing, he was acknowledging that he was not the one who had delivered them, but it was the Lord. He started well, but then the drift begins.

We see that although he refused power, he requested wealth. He said, "I do have one request, that each of you give me an earring from your share of the plunder" (8:24). The total weight of this gold was about 19.5 kilograms.[95] This was in addition to pendants and the chains that were on the necks of Midanites' camels. He became instantly wealthy!

What did he do with all that gold? He made it into an ephod and placed it in his hometown of Ophrah where it became an object of worship. The result was that this became a rival centre of worship to the Tabernacle which was in Shiloh. However, we

---

[94] Some of the thoughts of this section on Gideon were adapted from a sermon preached by Pastor John Musyimi, at AIC Ngong' Road, Nairobi on July 2, 2017 although I have not followed his interpretation entirely.

[95] Approximately $768,125 in today's valuation.

see no opposition from Gideon this time. Instead of saying, the Lord is the one you are to worship, he seems to drift along with or into this form of false worship.

Scripture goes on to tell us that Gideon had many wives and a concubine. Only the rich and powerful, like kings, could afford many wives. This could indicate a drift towards a kingly status and attitude and away from his declaration, "I will not rule over you." The writers at Bible.org state:

> Gideon retires and decides to live large. Verses 29-32 describe the lifestyle of a king, not that of a judge or a retired army officer. Gideon is quite wealthy, partly from the spoils of battle and partly from the gifts of the people. Often having too much stored away for retirement can be a bad thing. Wealth and leisure can destroy us. Instead of serving God, it is easy to squander some of the best years of our lives on ourselves. Are you building up God's kingdom or your own kingdom?[96]

This drift towards a king-like position could be further indicated by the name he gave to his son by his concubine: Abimelech. *Abimelech* means, "my father is king." Some scholars interpret it to mean "My (divine) Father is King." The NIV Study Bible says, "Gideon, in naming his son, acknowledges that the Lord (here called "Father") is King."[97] However, in light of this drift we see in Gideon's life and the fact that Abimelech killed off sixty-nine of his seventy brothers and induced his Canaanite family members to set him up as king (Judges 9), it may be that Gideon had drifted to this point exactly opposite from where he had started out.

---

[96] "From Great to Gone", Accessed July 2, 2017. https://bible.org/seriespage/5-great-gone-judges-822-957.

[97] *The NIV Study Bible* (Grand Rapids, Michigan: Zondervan Publishing House: 1985), 343.

life: The authors at Bible.org summarize the end of Gideon's life:

> It seems that Gideon's spectacular victory over the Midianites led to pride. Before long "Thy kingdom come" is replaced with "My kingdom come." Unfortunately, the old adage "Power corrupts; absolute power corrupts absolutely" often holds true even in the church. We must always bear in mind that those who are called to leadership in God's kingdom face constant temptation to exchange God's agenda for personal ambition and pleasure. Ironically, the more impressive one's achievements for God, the greater the temptation one may encounter. Please pray for your pastors, elders, and ministry leaders. Leaders are not immune to idolatry or immorality. In fact, we may be even more susceptible to these sins because of Satan's constant attack. We desperately need your prayers. *Greatness does not guarantee permanence* (emphasis theirs).[98]

What can we do so that we do not follow in the path of Gideon? What counters drifting with the currents of culture and custom that carry us away from God's call and commands? We need to keep our point of reference clearly in mind. When I was out in the lake, our place was easily identifiable because the retaining wall on the beach was painted with large green and white squares. It was unique from all of the other walls that lined the shore. It was unmistakable.

In the same way, we must continue to return to God's unique and unmistakable point of reference for our lives – his

---

98 "From Great to Gone".

revealed word in Scripture. Thus as our culture drifts we need to evaluate it and our participation in it from its unchanging perspective. We must remember that the Bible always judges culture; culture never judges the Bible.

We can be tempted to judge ourselves in our relative difference from our culture. The problem with this is that if we are ten units separated from our culture we may think we are doing well. However, if our culture drifts ten units towards evil and we then drift ten units in the same direction without realizing it we are now where the culture was earlier. We can illustrate it like this:

    Christian's   Culture's
    Position   Position

After drifting . . .

                Christian's   Culture's
                Position   Position

The Christian is now where the world previously was. Things that we would never accept or participate in earlier have now become accepted and practiced. And without care, the drifting will continue.

If we are in a boat, like I was as a young boy, we need to take up the oars and begin to row in the opposite direction. This takes effort and we have to be intentional about it. We will never go against the current and towards God if we don't steadfastly resist the inexorable undertow that pulls us away from him. If we continue to drift, we will never finish well!

Questions for Group and Personal Application:

1. Examine your life for areas where you have begun to drift. What do you think are steps you can take to regain the lost ground so you can return to your former position?

2. Put in your own words the warning in the statement, "Greatness does not guarantee permanence." How does this apply to your life?

3. Are you still growing, or have you plateaued?

CHAPTER 10

THE ISSUE OF INTENTIONALITY OR THE END IS THE BEGINNING

> "The hardest thing of all – to die rightly. – An exam nobody is spared – and how many pass it? And you?" [99]

> "The tragedy of life is not in the fact of death but what dies inside us while we live."[100]

Have you ever harboured wishes of being at your own funeral? Mark Twain told the story of the boy Tom Sawyer and two friends who ran away to become pirates. Twain detailed their adventures in the woods unknown to the people of the village. After a few days, they returned and hid in the balcony of the church just in time to hear their own funeral sermon which was filled with many wonderful things said about the young rascals. Twain wrote:

> As the service proceeded, the clergyman drew such pictures of the graces, the winning ways, and the rare promise of the lost lads

---

99 Dag Hammarskjöld, Leif Sjöberg and W. H. Auden, trans., *Markings* (New York: Alfred A. Knoph, 1964), 82

100 Cousins, Martin as quoted in Bob Benson and Michael W. Benson *Disciplines for the Inner Life.* (Waco, Texas: Word Books, 1985), 13.

that every soul there, thinking he recognized these pictures, felt a pang in remembering that he had persistently blinded himself to them always before, and had as persistently seen only faults and flaws in the poor boys. The minister related many a touching incident in the lives of the departed, too, which illustrated their sweet, generous natures, and the people could easily see, now, how noble and beautiful those episodes were, and remembered with grief that at the time they occurred they had seemed rank rascalities . . . [101]

Have you ever thought of what might be said at your own funeral? We might think imagining this is a bit morbid or strange. We might recoil from such thoughts. But, Dag Hammarskjöld had a different perspective when he wrote, "In the old days, Death was always one of the party. Now he sits next to me at the dinner table: I have to make friends with him."[102] Perhaps in the past, Death was always in the background or periphery of our perception, like an unfamiliar and unacquainted guest we casually ignored. But as we grow older, Death begins to move toward our inner circle and closer to us. His presence becomes more palpable; Death cannot be disregarded – so we must make friends with him. This may seem impossible, but for Christians death has lost its sting[103] and its fearfulness.[104]

How do we make friends with Death? For those who are believers in Christ, we see him as the one who will meet us at the end of our journey and convey us to our dearest friend,

---

101 Mark Twain, *The Adventures of Tom Sawyer* (Francson Classics: Kindle Edition, 2006) Kindle Locations 1523-1529).
102 Hammarskjöld, 106.
103 1 Corinthians 15:55.
104 Hebrews 2:15.

Life.[105] But what is Death's role now as our friend? He is here as an accountability partner. As we think of our mortality, and our desire to finish well, Death and his approach can inspire us to live the rest of our life in a manner worthy and pleasing of the Lord.

In light of Death's friendship and role as an accountability partner we need to be intentional about how we are going to finish our race. Thus, it would be profitable to reflect on what we would like people to highlight as they remembered us at our memorial service. Stephen Covey wrote:

> Now think deeply. What would you like each of these speakers to say about you and your life? What kind of husband, wife, father, or mother would you like their words to reflect? What kind of son or daughter or cousin? What kind of friend? What kind of working associate? What character would you like them to have seen in you? What contributions, what achievement would you want them to remember?[106]

In my seminars, I have often used the following adaptation of Lewis Carroll's story from Alice in Wonderland as an illustration of knowing what our goal is before we set out on our journey:

> A traveller came to a fork in the road. He asked an old man, "Which road do I take?"
> "Where do you want to go?' responded the other.
> "I don't know." The traveller answered.
> "Then," said the old man, "it doesn't matter."[107]

---

105 Of course, this is Jesus who said, I am the Way, the Truth and the Life! (John 14:6). Norman Cousins,

106 Stephen R. Covey, The 7 Habits of Highly Effective People: Restoring the Character Ethic (New York: Free Press, 2004), 97.

107 Adapted from Lewis Carroll, Alice's Adventures in Wonderland (Seattle: AmazonClassics, n.d.), 42. Kindle. Carroll's original lines are:
"Would you tell me, please, which way I ought to go from here?" "That depends a good deal on where you want to get to," said the Cat. "I don't much care where—" said Alice. "Then it doesn't matter which way you go," said the Cat.

Unfortunately, many people live their lives with no thought of where they are going. They have no idea of what the end of the journey might be. They are so absorbed in day-to-day living, the struggle to survive, their work, and their pleasures, that the question of how they will finish does not seem to enter their consciousness. Others just drift through life, one day at a time slipping away, without reflecting on its value or its contribution to the quality of their lives or the legacy they may leave behind.

But if our end goal is that of finishing well, shouldn't we be giving it some thought now? In other words, what is our vision for the rest of our lives so that we can finish well? Stephen Farrar addressed this:

> What does it mean to finish strong? It means that you will come to the end of your life with a strong and close relationship to Christ. It means that, unless God has taken your wife ahead of you, you will be married to the same woman that you are today. It means that you are a man who is in the Scriptures and living the Scriptures. It means that you are a man who has fought some battles for the kingdom and has the scars to prove it. To finish strong means that you are leaving your children and grandchildren the *priceless* heritage of a godly life (emphasis his).
>
> *To do that takes vision* (emphasis mine). Especially if you are in your twenties or thirties. Few men have the vision at that age to look forty years into the future and think about how they want to finish.[108]

---

108 Farrar, 215.

Recently, I was discussing with a friend, the idea of finishing well as a missionary in Kenya. He asked me, "What would that look like?" As we discussed the next few years, it became evident that there were still some responsibilities and projects that I would like to fulfil and finish. These have now become, more than ever, the focus of my life and ministry. I have an end goal in sight. I know where I am heading and what I believe God wants me to achieve.

These tangible goals are easy to spell out, especially as compared to the character and spiritual goals that I still need to work on until my earthly time is finished. These attribute goals are harder to put down in objective form, but I need to do it carefully and prayerfully if I will finish well in my personal life and walk with God. Stephen Covey pointed out the importance of the end goal when he wrote:

> [To] "begin with the end in mind" is to begin today with the image, picture, or paradigm of the end of your life as your frame of reference or the criterion by which everything else is examined. Each part of your life – today's behaviour, tomorrow's behaviour, next week's behaviour, next month's behaviour – can be examined in the context of the whole, of what really matters most to you. By keeping that end clearly in mind, you can make certain that whatever you do on any particular day does not violate the criteria you have defined as supremely important, and that each day of your life contributes in a meaningful way to the vision you have of your life as a whole.

To begin with the end in mind means to start with a clear understanding of your destination. It means to know where you're going so you can better understand where you are now and so that the steps you take are always in the right direction.[109]

What does this require? It requires that we must slow down enough to take the time to think about our life and the direction we are headed. We must ask ourselves, *When I arrive at the end of my life, where do I want to be? Where do I want to be in terms of my relationship with God? In terms of my relationships with my family, friends, society? Where do I want to be in terms of my achievements? Where do I want to be in the development of my character?*

Without asking these questions and setting out to do something about them we will not finish well. We will end up falling far short of what God intended us to be and to do. This journey is an exploration of our interior being. It is an expedition to the core of our soul and who we really are. And it is not short or easy. As Dag Hammarskjöld wrote:

The longest journey is the journey inwards.[110]

May I encourage you to take time to carefully work through these questions? There is a "Finishing Well Questionnaire" at the back of this book. This will take some time and careful prayerful thought but it may bring to the surface issues that you will need to address if you are going to finish well.

From this Point On – Finish Well!

Part of finishing well is living well – now! As my mother-in-law said to her daughters, "If you want to be a sweet lady when you are old, you need to start being a sweet lady now." These words of Thomas à Kempis can encourage us:

---

109 Covey, 98.
110 Hammarskjöld, 58.

> My brother, lose not your confidence of making progress towards the things of the Spirit; you still have time, the hours is not yet past (Romans 13:11; Hebrews 10:35). Why will you defer your good purpose from day to day? Arise and in this very instant begin, and say, Now is the time to be doing, now is the time to be fighting, now is the time to be amending myself.[111]

It does not matter where you are in your spiritual pilgrimage. You may be young and you have visions and plans for a long life of ministry. Or you may be further down the path, and life has had its share of disappointment, disillusionment, and defeat. God is the God of the second chance. God is the God of grace. You can finish well from this point on!

T.S. Eliot wrote, "Old men ought to be explorers."[112] Kenyan educator, lawyer, civil rights activist, politician, and author Kivutha Kibwana demonstrated this when he wrote of his own spiritual journey to faith. In his book *Walk With Me, God* he expressed his desire to finish well even though he had started his quest later in life. He wrote:

> Is it too late for me to gradually and surely build my relationship with you and my faith in you? You must help me lean on you . . . I know I have wasted four decades in which I could have become a seasoned follower of Christ. I could have matured in the Lord. I am happy though you have shown me the way at this time. Others continue with a feeble, weak-kneed faith until their death. You have decided that will not be my plight. You are

---

111 à Kempis, 49.
112 T.S. Eliot, as quoted by Hammarskjöld, 62.

> responsible for my wake up call, Lord . . . You have given me a second chance . . . I will now more or less start afresh, all over again.[113]

Therefore, no matter where you are in your relationship with God, today is the day to determine to finish well. As Covey said, "When people seriously undertake to identify what really matters most to them in their lives, what they really want to be and do, they become very reverent. They start to think in larger terms than today and tomorrow."[114] Thomas á Kempis added:

> We ought to daily renew our purpose and to stir up ourselves to fervour, as though we had for the first time today entered the Christian life, and to say: "Help me, O Lord God, in this my good purpose and in Thy holy service." . . . According to our purpose shall be the course of our spiritual profiting; and much diligence is necessary to him who will profit much.[115]

Therefore, let me encourage you that today is the day you can start afresh with the Lord. It is never too late to start the process of finishing well.

Where Is the Finish Line?

The simple answer is we don't know. It is different for each one of us. This is what the author implied when he wrote: "Let us run with perseverance the race marked out *for us*" (Hebrews 12:1, emphasis mine). This is what Thomas à Kempis in his chapter "Meditation on Death" encourages us to do:

---

113 Kivutha Kibwana, *Walk With Me, God* (Nairobi: Word Alive Publishers, 2009), 70.
114 Covey, 132.
115 à Kempis, 39.

Oh, dullness and hardness of man's heart, which thinks only upon the present, and does not rather care for what is to come! You ought so to order yourself in every act and thought, as if today you were on the point to die . . . Blessed is he who always has the hour of his death before his eyes (Ecclesiastes 7:1), and daily prepares himself to die. If at any time you have seen another man die, remember you must also pass the same way (Hebrews 9:27). When it is morning, think you might not come to eventide. And when it is evening, dare not to promise yourself the morning. Always, therefore, be ready, and so live that death may never take you unprepared for many die suddenly. When that last hour shall come, you will have a far different opinion of your whole past life and regret you have been so careless and remiss.

How wise and happy is he who now labours to be in life as he wishes to be found at his death![116]

Dag Hammarskjöld adds: "Do not seek death. Death will find you. But seek the road which makes death a fulfilment."[117] The application to those of us who desire to finish well is this: We don't know when our race will end. Therefore, to finish well we must live each day well. There is no better day to start than today!

---

116 à Kempis, 51-52.
117 Hammarskjöld, 159.

Questions for Group and Personal Application:

When you arrive at the end of your life, where do you want to be in terms of these questions?

1. Where do I want to be in terms of my relationship with God?

2. Where do I want to be in terms of my relationships with my family, friends, and society?

3. Where do I want to be in terms of my achievements?

4. Where do I want to be in the development of my character?

To answer these questions, follow the "Finishing Well questionnaire at the end of this book.

EPILOGUE

"And what more shall I say? I do not have time to tell about . . . Samson . . . who through faith . . . (Hebrews 11:32-33a)."

After studying the life of Samson as recorded in Judges it seems almost strange to see him commended (Hebrews 11:39) for his faith. Where do we see his faith demonstrated? I believe we can see it in at least two significant events in his life. The first was when the men of Judea turned him over to the Philistines (Judges 15:9-13).

I believe the Spirit of God came upon Samson because when he yielded himself as a prisoner to the men of Judah, he exercised faith. He didn't want to fight and hurt his own people. Because he knew God's promise that he would begin to deliver his people from the Philistines, he trusted God to take care of him even if he was handed over to his enemies. God did just that and he was able to defeat the Philistines who had come to kill him.

After the battle, when he was literally "dying of thirst" he again called out in faith to God for help. And God heard him. God was there for him and because of his faith he helped him in his time of need.

The second event was when he prayed to receive his strength back as he stood between the two supporting pillars in the Philistine temple (Judges 16:28). This too seems strange, as his motive was one more act of revenge and to be avenged of the loss of his eyes. Gleason L. Archer commented on this passage:

> In a sense he ended his earthly career (after a long period of penitence for his previous folly and immorality) by one magnificent "act of righteousness" (Judges 16:33), when he pulled down the pillars of the temple of Dagon on the jeering crowd of Philistines, as they derided their blinded captive and his "powerless" God. Samson was willing to give up his own life in the interests of his nation and his Lord – even though part of his motivation was vengeance on his tormentors for putting out his eyes.[118]

This raises the question, what was the nature of Samson's faith? Oswald Chambers gave us a clue when he described the nature of faith: "Faith is the heroic effort of your life, *you fling yourself in reckless confidence on God*"[119] (emphasis mine). Pulling down the Philistine temple upon oneself can be nothing more than that. He was flinging his eternal destiny in reckless confidence on God.

Samson's inclusion in the "Hall of Faith" says to us at least two important things. First, Scripture does not tell us everything that we would like to know about a person's life. Instead, the Bible

---

[118] Gleason L. Archer, *Encyclopedia of Bible Difficulties* (Grand Rapids, Michigan: Zondervan Publishing House, 1982), 421.

[119] Oswald Chambers, 93.

is selective in what it records. As such, Samson's life stands more as an example to us of wasted potential and wantonness. It is a warning against the lusts of the flesh instead of an example of a life of faith and faithfulness to emulate.

Secondly, we must see in the apostle's commentary on this judge's record an aspect of the mysterious nature of God. From a human standpoint, one would expect to see members of this list of heroes of faith to be people of exemplary character and faithfulness. And yet Samson was not.

The truth is that God values faith – even faith as small as a mustard seed – even faith that is exercised at the end of one's life such as that of the thief who was crucified with Jesus. And when we exercise that faith we receive God's unmerited grace. Ultimately, this can be of great encouragement to us in our own spiritual journey and life of faith. If God found faith in the brokenness of Samson's life, surely there is hope for us as well. The Puritan wrote:

> Help me to see that it is faith stirred by grace that does the deed, that faith brings a man nearer to thee, raising him above mere men, that thou dost act upon the soul when thus elevated and lifted out of itself, that faith centres in thee as God all-sufficient.[120]

In the movie series, *The Band of Brothers,* there is an episode which chronicles the failed "Market Garden" invasion of the allies into Holland during World War II. At first they meet with great success and are greeted as liberators by the joyful population. Soon the American soldiers watch in amazement as certain women are stripped of their dresses, shorn of their hair, and marked with

---
[120] Bennet, 330-331.

a black Nazi swastika on their foreheads. When the soldiers ask why, they are told that the women had slept with the enemy.

As the army is retreating, one of those shamed women stands beside the road, holding a baby. The soldiers eye her with stony silence. She waits silently, humiliated, helpless, and hopeless as the column of troops passed by. Then without saying a word, one of the soldiers reaches into his kit, takes out a box of biscuits and hands it to her in an act of undeserved mercy and grace.

Samson, in the Philistine temple had been shorn of his hair, blinded, had lost his dignity, and been totally humiliated. Yet despite his weaknesses, his failures, his sleeping with the enemy, he found grace in the eyes of the Lord. He did not deserve to receive his strength back for one more great effort. His behaviour deserved the punishment of the grinding mill for the rest of his life. And yet, in faith he cried out to God and received his grace! Herbert Lockyer commented on this:

> Out of the depths Samson cried unto the Lord, and, as we read, his hair began to grow. Forsaken by all, there was One near at hand, and the God of grace restored unto His sinning and now repentant servant, the power he had lost. Samson's extremity became God's opportunity.[121]

The same is true for us. We are sinners, traitors, and collaborators with the enemy. Yet, God's richest grace is available for us when we cry out to him in faith. This is the way of hope! It is through God's grace that we can finish well! Therefore we can be encouraged by Thomas à Kempis's words:

---

[121] Herbert Lockyer, *All the Women of the Bible* (Grand Rapids, Michigan: Zondervan Publishing House, n.d.), 43-44.

Be on your guard against self-complacency and pride; for it is through these that many are led into error, and sometimes into an almost incurable blindness of soul. Let the downfall of those who foolishly rely on themselves be a warning to you and keep you always humble. Fight on like a good soldier; and if sometimes through weakness you fall, get up again and with greater strength than before, *trust in [the Lord's] abundant grace* (emphasis mine).[122]

As the hymn writer said:

> Marvellous grace of our loving Lord, grace that exceeds our sin and our guilt, yonder on Calvary's mount out-poured, there where the blood of the Lamb was spilt.
>
> Sin and despair, like the sea waves cold, Threaten the soul with infinite loss; Grace that is greater, yes, grace untold, Points to the refuge, the mighty cross.
>
> Dark is the stain that we cannot hide, what can avail to wash it away! Look! there is flowing a crimson tide; whiter than snow you may be today.
>
> Marvellous, infinite, matchless grace, freely bestowed on all who believe; you that are longing to see his face, will you this moment his grace receive?
>
> Refrain: Grace, grace, God's grace, grace that will pardon and cleanse within; grace, grace, God's grace, grace that is greater than all our sin.[123]

---

122 Thomas à Kempis, Claire L. Fitzpatrick, ed., *The Imitation of Christ* (New York: Catholic Book Publishing Co., 1985), 125. I have arranged the order of the sentences and combined them into one paragraph.

123 Julia H. Johnston, "Grace Greater Than Our Sin" in *The Hymnal for Worship & Celebration* (Waco, Texas: Word Music, 1986), 201.

FINISHING WELL QUESTIONNAIRE[124]

Someone gave me a folder from the Catholic Relief Services and I put this questionnaire inside it when I took a spiritual retreat to work through the questions. As I glanced at the cover I saw the following: Faith. Action. Results. I thought how fitting these words were for this exercise. Let me ask you to answer these questions in faith trusting God to help you hear his voice. Then in that attitude of faith take each action God has laid on your heart. And then in faith believe that God will bring about the results that you trust him for.

Prayerfully and carefully answer these questions from the perspective of what you would like to be in each of these areas at the end or your life.

1. What kind of child of God do you want to be?
    - What steps are you going to take to become this?

---

[124] Some of the questions have been adapted from Stephen R. Covey, *The 7 Habits of Highly Effective People: Restoring the Character Ethic* (New York: Free Press, 2004), 97.

2. What kind of husband/wife do you want to be?
   - What steps are you going to take to become this?
3. What kind of father/mother do want to be?
   - What steps are you going to take to become this?
4. What kind of son/daughter do you want to be?
   - What steps are you going to take to become this?
5. What kind of friend do you want to be?
   - What steps are you going to take to become this?
6. What kind of working associate do you want to be?
   - What steps are you going to take to become this?
7. What character qualities do you want to improve or develop?
   - What steps are you going to take to develop these qualities?
8. What contributions do want to make?
   - What steps are you going to take to make these contributions?
9. What achievements would you like accomplish?
   - What steps are you going to take to accomplish these goals?
10. What else might God be bringing to your mind and heart to do to finish **well**?
    - What steps are you going to take to make this become a reality?

WORKS CITED

à Kempis, Thomas, *The Imitation of Christ.* Chicago: Moody Press, 1982.

à Kempis, Thomas, *The Imitation of Christ.* Xist Classics, Ignatius Press, Kindle Edition.

à Kempis, Thomas, Claire L. Fitzpatrick, ed., *The Imitation of Christ.* New York: Catholic Book Publishing Co., 1985.

Archer, Gleason L., *Encyclopedia of Bible Difficulties.* Grand Rapids, Michigan: Zondervan Publishing House, 1982.

Aterburn, Stephen and Fred Stoeker, *Everyman's Battle.* Colorado Springs, Colorado: Waterbrook Press, 2000.

Baxter, Richard, *The Reformed Pastor.* New York: American Tract Society, n.d.

Bennett, Arthur, *The Valley of Vision.* Edinburgh: The Banner of Truth Trust, 2006.

Carroll, Lewis. *Alice's Adventures in Wonderland.* Seattle, Amazon Classics, n.d. Kindle.

Chambers, Oswald, *My Utmost for His Highest*. Uhrichsville, Ohio: Barbour and Company, Inc., n.d.

Chambers. Oswald, *My Utmost for His Highest*, Updated Edition (Kindle Locations 4294-4300). Discovery House. Kindle Edition.

Chesterton, G. K., *St. Francis of Assisi*. Veritatis Splendor Publications, 2013. Kindle.

Clinton, J. Robert, *The Making of a Leader*. Colorado Springs, Colorado: NavPress, 1988.

Cousins, Martin in Bob Benson and Michael W. Benson *Disciplines for the Inner Life*. Waco, Texas: Word Books, 1985.

Covey, Stephen R., *The 7 Habits of Highly Effective People: Restoring the Character Ethic*. New York: Free Press, 2004.

Cunningham, Sarah, *Dear Church*. Grand Rapids, Michigan: Zondervan, 2006.

Duffield, Jr., George, "Stand Up, Stand Up for Jesus" in *The Hymnal for Worship & Celebration*. Waco, Texas: Word Music, 1986.

Farrar, Steve, *Finishing Strong*. Colorado Springs, Colorado: Multnomah Books, 1995.

"From Great to Gone." Accessed July 2, 2017. https://bible.org/seriespage/5-great-gone-judges-822-957.

Hammarsköld, Dag, Leif Sjöberg and W. H. Auden, trans., *Markings*. New York: Alfred A. Knoph, 1964.

"How Many Pastors Are Addicted to Porn? The Stats are Surprising." Accessed February 1, 2017. http://www.expastors.com/how-many-pastors-are-addicted-to-porn-the-stats-are-surprising/.

Hybels, Bill, *Honest to God*. Grand Rapids, Michigan: Zondervan Publishing House, 1992.

Johnston, Julia H. "Grace Greater Than Our Sin" in *The Hymnal for Worship & Celebration* Waco, Texas: Word Music, 1986

Jones, L. Gregory, *Embodying Forgiveness*. Grand Rapids, Michigan: William B. Eerdmans Publishing Company, 1995.

Jones, L. Gregory and Célestin Mussekura, *Forgiving as We've Been Forgiven*. Downers Grove, Illinois: InterVarsity Press, 2010.

Kryger, Steven, "Accountability Software – Comparing 5 of the Best Tools," Accessed July 5, 2017. http://www.communicatejesus.com/accountability-software-comparison/.

------"Don't Fear ISIS-Fear Your iPhone." Accessed July 5, 2017. http://www.communicatejesus.com/dont-fear-isis-fear-iphone/.

Lewis, Milton, *Sundays with Scottie*. Siloam Springs, Arkansas: Leafwood Publishers, 2003.

"Ligonier Suspends R.S. Sproul, Jr. Over Ashley Madison." Accessed September 14, 2015. http://www.christianitytoday.com/gleanings/2015/august/ligonier-suspends-rc-sproul-jr-over-ashley-madison.html.

Lockyer, Herbert, *All the Men of the Bible*. Grand Rapids, Michigan: Zondervan Publishing House, 1958.

------*All the Women of the Bible*. Grand Rapids, Michigan: Zondervan Publishing House, n.d.

Martin, W.B.J., *Little Sins, Big Consequences*. Nashville, Tennessee: Abingdon Press, 1982.

Morley, Patrick *The Man in the Mirror.* Grand Rapids, Michigan: Zondervan Publishing House, 1997.

NIV Study Bible. Grand Rapids, Michigan: Zondervan Publishing House: 1985.

Pollard, A. F., *King Henry VIII, An Illustrated Biography.* Shamrock Eden Publishing. Kindle Edition.

Robinson, Robert "Come Thou Fount" in *The Hymnal for Worship & Celebration.* Waco, Texas: Word Music, 1986.

Roberts, Mark D., *Dare to Be True.* Colorado Springs, Colorado: Waterbrook Press, 2003.

Tolentino, Jia "On the Origin of Certain Quotable 'African Proverbs'." Accessed July 30, 2017. http://jezebel.com/on-the-origin-of-certain-quotable-african-proverbs-1766664089.

Turnbull, Ralph G., *A Minister's Obstacles.* New York: Fleming H. Revell, 1946.

Twain, Mark. *The Adventures of Tom Sawyer.* Francson Classics, 2006. Kindle.

Volf, Miroslav, *Exclusion and Embrace.* Nashville, Tennessee: Abingdon Press, 1996.

"What the Heart Loves the Will Chooses." Accessed May 7, 2017. http://www.goodreads.com/quotes/528599-what-the-heart-loves-the-will-chooses-and-the-mind.

Wood, Leon, *The Distressing Days of the Judges.* Grand Rapids, Michigan: Zondervan Publishing House, 1976.

Experience the truth and beauty of *God's Word Through African Eye*s.

With notes written by over **350 contributors** from **50 countries** in **five major languages**, the *Africa Study Bible*™ is a collaboration of scholars, leaders, pastors, and teachers from across the continent, who together created **the most ethnically diverse, single-volume, biblical resource to date.**

Discover more at **africastudybible.com**.

OASIS INTERNATIONAL LIMITED
Satisfying Africa's Thirst for God's Word

africastudybible.com
facebook.com/africastudybible
info@oasisint.net

NLT.
The Truth Made
CLEAR

OASIS INTERNATIONAL

is the proud publisher
of many great titles to help inform your Christian life!
Visit oasisint.net to learn more.

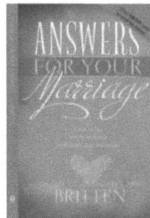 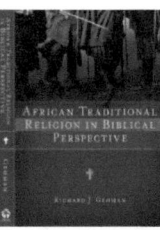 

Answers for your Marriage
Bruce & Carol Britten

African Traditional Religion
in Biblical Perspective
Richard Gehman

A Pre-Marriage Counselling
Handbook
Alan & Donna Goerz

African Traditional Religion
and Christian Counseling
Karl Grebe & Wilfred Fon

Learning to Lead
Richard Gehman

Biblical Christianity in
African Perspective
Wilber O'Donovan

Conflict Resolution
in the Church
Philip Morrison & Chris Mwala'a

  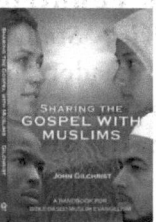

Love & Marriage
Bruce & Carol Britten

Biblical Christianity in
Modern Africa
Wilber O'Donovan

Sharing the Gospel with
Muslims
John Gilchrist

OASIS INTERNATIONAL LIMITED
Satisfying Africa's Thirst for God's Word

oasisint.net
facebook.com/OasisIntLtd
info@oasisint.net

Printed by Libri Plureos GmbH in Hamburg, Germany